Fortinet NSE 4 7.2 Actual Exam Actual Questions

Fortinet Network Security Professional 4

Stefan Meirelles

Question: 1

Which two statements are correct about NGFW Policy-based mode? (Choose two.)

A. NGFW policy-based mode does not require the use of central source NAT policy
B. NGFW policy-based mode can only be applied globally and not on individual VDOMs
C. NGFW policy-based mode supports creating applications and web filtering categories directly in a firewall policy
D. NGFW policy-based mode policies support only flow inspection

Answer: CD

Question: 2

Refer to the exhibit.

```
session info: proto=6 proto_state=02 duration=6 expire=6 timeout=3600 flags=0000
0000 socktype=0 sockport=0 av_idx=0 use=3
origin-shaper=
reply-shaper=
per_ip_shaper=
class_id=0 ha_id=0 policy_dir=0 tunnel=/ vlan_cos=0/255
state=may_dirty
statistic(bytes/packets/allow_err): org=180/3/1 reply=264/3/1 tuples=2
tx speed(Bps/kbps): 26/0 rx speed(Bps/kbps): 39/0
orgin->sink: org pre->post, reply pre->post dev=3->5/5->3 gwy=10.0.1.11/0.0.0.0
hook=pre dir=org act=dnat 10.200.3.1:38024->10.200.1.11:80(10.0.1.11:80)
hook=post dir=reply act=snat 10.0.1.11:80->10.200.3.1:38024(10.200.1.11:80)
pos/(before,after) 0/(0,0), 0/(0,0)
misc=0 policy_id=8 auth_info=0 chk_client_info=0 vd=0
serial=0001fb06 tos=ff/ff app_list=0 app=0 url_cat=0
rpdb_link_id= 00000000 rpdb_svc_id=0 ngfwid=n/a
npu_state=0x040000
```

Which contains a session diagnostic output. Which statement is true about the session diagnostic output?

A. The session is in SYN_SeNT state.
B. The session is in FIN_ACK state.
C. The session is in FTN_WAIT state.
D. The session is in eSTABLISHeD state.

Answer: A

Indicates TCP (proto=6) session in SYN_SeNT state (proto=state=2)

https://kb.fortinet.com/kb/viewContent.do?externalId=FD30042

Question: 3

Which two statements explain antivirus scanning modes? (Choose two.)

A. In proxy-based inspection mode, files bigger than the buffer size are scanned.
B. In flow-based inspection mode, FortiGate buffers the file, but also simultaneously transmits it to the client.
C. In proxy-based inspection mode, antivirus scanning buffers the whole file for scanning, before sending it to the client.
D. In flow-based inspection mode, files bigger than the buffer size are scanned.

Answer: BC

An antivirus profile in full scan mode buffers up to your specified file size limit. The default is 10 MB.

That is large enough for most files, except video files. If your FortiGate model has more RAM, you may be able to increase this threshold. Without a limit, very large files could exhaust the scan memory. So, this threshold balances risk and performance. Is this tradeoff unique to

FortiGate, or to a specific model? No. Regardless of vendor or model, you must make a choice. This is because of the difference between scans in theory, that have no limits, and scans on real-world devices, that have finite RAM. In order to detect 100% of malware regardless of file size, a firewall would need infinitely large RAM--something that no device has in the real world. Most viruses are very small.

This table shows a typical tradeoff. You can see that with the default 10 MB threshold, only 0.01% of viruses pass through.

Question: 4

Refer to the web filter raw logs.

```
date=2020-07-09 time=12:51:51 logid="0316013057" type="utm"
subtype="webfilter" eventtype="ftgd_blk" level="warning"
vd="root" eventtime=1594313511250173744 tz="-0400" policyid=1
sessionid=5526 srcip=10.0.1.10 srcport=48660 srcintf="port2"
srcintfrole="undefined" dstip=104.244.42.193 dstport=443
dstintf="port1" dstintfrole="undefined" proto=6 service="HTTPS"
hostname="twitter.com" profile="all_users_web" action="blocked"
reqtype="direct" url="https://twitter.com/" sentbyte=517
rcvdbyte=0 direction="outgoing" msg="URL belongs to a category
with warnings enabled" method="domain" cat=37 catdesc="Social
Networking"

date=2020-07-09 time=12:52:16 logid="0316013057" type="utm"
subtype="webfilter" eventtype="ftgd_blk" level="warning"
vd="root" eventtime=1594313537024536428 tz="-0400" policyid=1
sessionid=5552 srcip=10.0.1.10 srcport=48698 srcintf="port2"
srcintfrole="undefined" dstip=104.244.42.193 dstport=443
dstintf="port1" dstintfrole="undefined" proto=6 service="HTTPS"
hostname="twitter.com" profile="all_users_web"
action="passthrough" reqtype="direct" url="https://twitter.com/"
sentbyte=369 rcvdbyte=0 direction="outgoing" msg="URL belongs to
a category with warnings enabled" method="domain" cat=37
catdesc="Social Networking"
```

Based on the raw logs shown in the exhibit, which statement is correct?

A. Social networking web filter category is configured with the action set to authenticate.

B. The action on firewall policy ID 1 is set to warning.

C. Access to the social networking web filter category was explicitly blocked to all users.
D. The name of the firewall policy is all_users_web.

Answer: A

Question: 5

Which two configuration settings are synchronized when FortiGate devices are in an active-active HA cluster? (Choose two.)

A. FortiGuard web filter cache
B. FortiGate hostname
C. NTP
D. DNS

Answer: CD

Question: 6

An administrator wants to configure timeouts for users. Regardless of the userTMs behavior, the timer should start as soon as the user authenticates and expire after the configured value.

Which timeout option should be configured on FortiGate?

A. auth-on-demand
B. soft-timeout
C. idle-timeout
D. new-session
E. hard-timeout

Answer: e

Reference:

https://kb.fortinet.com/kb/documentLink.do?externalID=FD37221#:~:text=Hard%20timeout%3A%20User%20

Question: 7

Why does FortiGate Keep TCP sessions in the session table for several seconds, even after both sides (client and server) have terminated the session?

A. To allow for out-of-order packets that could arrive after the FIN/ACK packets
B. To finish any inspection operations
C. To remove the NAT operation
D. To generate logs

Answer: A

TCP provides the ability for one end of a connection to terminate its output while still receiving data from the other end. This is called a half-close. FortiGate unit implements a specific timer before removing an entry in the firewall session table.

Question: 8

Which two protocols are used to enable administrator access of a FortiGate device? (Choose two.)

A. SSH
B. HTTPS
C. FTM

D. FortiTelemetry

Answer: AB

Reference:

https://docs.fortinet.com/document/fortigate/6.4.0/hardening-yourfortigate/995103/buildingsecurity-into-fortios

Question: 9

Refer to the exhibit.

```
# diagnose test application ipsmonitor
1: Display IPS engine information
2: Toggle IPS engine enable/disable status
3: Display restart log
4: Clear restart log
5: Toggle bypass status
98: Stop all IPS engines
99: Restart all IPS engines and monitor
```

examine the intrusion prevention system (IPS) diagnostic command.

Which statement is correct If option 5 was used with the IPS diagnostic command and the outcome was a decrease in the CPU usage?

A. The IPS engine was inspecting high volume of traffic.
B. The IPS engine was unable to prevent an intrusion attack .
C. The IPS engine was blocking all traffic.
D. The IPS engine will continue to run in a normal state.

Answer: A

Reference:

https://docs.fortinet.com/document/fortigate/6.2.3/cookbook/232929/troubleshooting-high-cpuusage

Question: 10

By default, FortiGate is configured to use HTTPS when performing live web filtering with FortiGuard servers. Which CLI command will cause FortiGate to use an unreliable protocol to communicate with FortiGuard servers for live web filtering?

A. set fortiguard-anycast disable
B. set webfilter-force-off disable
C. set webfilter-cache disable
D. set protocol tcp

Answer: A

By default, "fortiguard-anycast" is enabled, and this setting only works with "set protocol https". To use udp (ie. "set protocol udp"), "fortiguard-anycast" must be disabled.

"By default, FortiGate is configured to enforce the use of HTTPS port 443 to perform live filtering with FortiGuard or FortiManager. Other ports and protocols are available by disabling the FortiGuard anycast setting on the CLI."

Question: 11

How does FortiGate act when using SSL VPN in web mode?

A. FortiGate acts as an FDS server.
B. FortiGate acts as an HTTP reverse proxy.

C. FortiGate acts as DNS server.
D. FortiGate acts as router.

Answer: B

Reference:

https://pub.kb.fortinet.com/ksmcontent/Fortinet-Public/current/Fortigate_v4.0MR3/fortigatesslvpn-40-mr3.pdf

Question: 12

Which three statements explain a flow-based antivirus profile? (Choose three.)

A. IPS engine handles the process as a standalone.
B. FortiGate buffers the whole file but transmits to the client simultaneously.
C. If the virus is detected, the last packet is delivered to the client.
D. Optimized performance compared to proxy-based inspection.
E. Flow-based inspection uses a hybrid of scanning modes available in proxy-based inspection.

Answer: BDe

Reference:

https://forum.fortinet.com/tm.aspx?m=192309

Question: 13

Refer to the exhibits to view the firewall policy (exhibit A) and the antivirus profile (exhibit B).

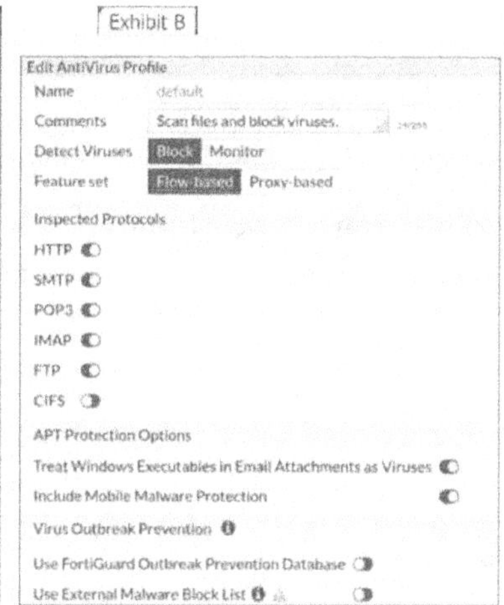

Which statement is correct if a user is unable to receive a block replacement message when downloading an infected file for the first time?

A. The firewall policy performs the full content inspection on the file.
B. The flow-based inspection is used, which resets the last packet to the user.
C. The volume of traffic being inspected is too high for this model of FortiGate.
D. The intrusion prevention security profile needs to be enabled when using flow-based inspection mode.

Answer: B

· "ONLY" If the virus is detected at the "START" of the connection, the IPS engine sends the block replacement message immediately

· When a virus is detected on a TCP session (FIRST TIMe), but where "SOMe PACKeTS" have been already forwarded to the receiver, FortiGate "resets the connection" and does not send the last piece of the file. Although the receiver got most of the file content, the file has been truncated and therefore, can't be opened. The IPS engine also caches the URL of the infected file, so that if a "SeCOND ATTeMPT" to transmit the file is made, the IPS engine will then send a block replacement message to the client instead of scanning the file again.

In flow mode, the FortiGate drops the last packet killing the file. But because of that the block replacement message cannot be displayed. If the file is attempted to download again the block message will be shown.

Question: 14

A network administrator wants to set up redundant IPsec VPN tunnels on FortiGate by using two IPsec VPN tunnels and static routes.

* All traffic must be routed through the primary tunnel when both tunnels are up

* The secondary tunnel must be used only if the primary tunnel goes down

* In addition, FortiGate should be able to detect a dead tunnel to speed up tunnel failover Which two key configuration changes are needed on FortiGate to meet the design requirements? (Choose two,)

A. Configure a high distance on the static route for the primary tunnel, and a lower distance on the static route for the secondary tunnel.
B. enable Dead Peer Detection.
C. Configure a lower distance on the static route for the primary tunnel, and a higher distance on the static route for the secondary tunnel.
D. enable Auto-negotiate and Autokey Keep Alive on the phase 2 configuration of both tunnels.

Answer: BC

Study Guide – IPsec VPN – IPsec configuration – Phase 1 Network.

When Dead Peer Detection (DPD) is enabled, DPD probes are sent to detect a failed tunnel and bring it down before its IPsec SAs expire. This failure detection mechanism is very useful when you have redundant paths to the same destination, and you want to failover to a backup connection when the primary connection fails to keep the connectivity between the sites up.

There are three DPD modes. On demand is the default mode.

Study Guide – IPsec VPN – Redundant VPNs.

Add one phase 1 configuration for each tunnel. DPD should be enabled on both ends.

Add at least one phase 2 definition for each phase 1.

Add one static route for each path. Use distance or priority to select primary routes over backup routes (routes for the primary VPN must have a lower distance or lower priority than the backup). Alternatively, use dynamic routing. Configure FW policies for each IPsec interface.

Question: 15

Which engine handles application control traffic on the next-generation firewall (NGFW) FortiGate?

A. Antivirus engine
B. Intrusion prevention system engine
C. Flow engine
D. Detection engine

Answer: B

http://docs.fortinet.com/document/fortigate/6.0.0/handbook/240599/application-control

Reference:
http://docs.fortinet.com/document/fortigate/6.0.0/handbook/240599/applicationcontrol

Question: 16

Refer to the exhibit.

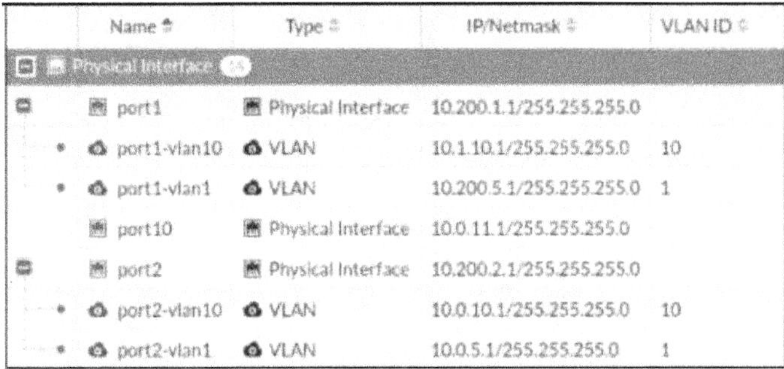

Name	Type	IP/Netmask	VLAN ID
Physical Interface			
port1	Physical Interface	10.200.1.1/255.255.255.0	
port1-vlan10	VLAN	10.1.10.1/255.255.255.0	10
port1-vlan1	VLAN	10.200.5.1/255.255.255.0	1
port10	Physical Interface	10.0.11.1/255.255.255.0	
port2	Physical Interface	10.200.2.1/255.255.255.0	
port2-vlan10	VLAN	10.0.10.1/255.255.255.0	10
port2-vlan1	VLAN	10.0.5.1/255.255.255.0	1

Given the interfaces shown in the exhibit. which two statements are true? (Choose two.)

A. Traffic between port2 and port2-vlan1 is allowed by default.
B. port1-vlan10 and port2-vlan10 are part of the same broadcast domain.
C. port1 is a native VLAN.
D. port1-vlan and port2-vlan1 can be assigned in the same VDOM or to different VDOMs.

Answer: CD

https://community.fortinet.com/t5/FortiGate/Technical-Tip-rules-about-VLAN-configuration-andVDOM-interf

https://kb.fortinet.com/kb/viewContent.do?externalId=FD30883

Question: 17

A. Which statement about video filtering on FortiGate is true?
B. Full SSL Inspection is not required.
C. It is available only on a proxy-based firewall policy.
D. It inspects video files hosted on file sharing services.

E. Video filtering FortiGuard categories are based on web filter FortiGuard categories.

Answer: B

Reference: https://docs.fortinet.com/document/fortigate/7.0.0/new-features/190873/video-filtering

Question: 18

Refer to the exhibit.

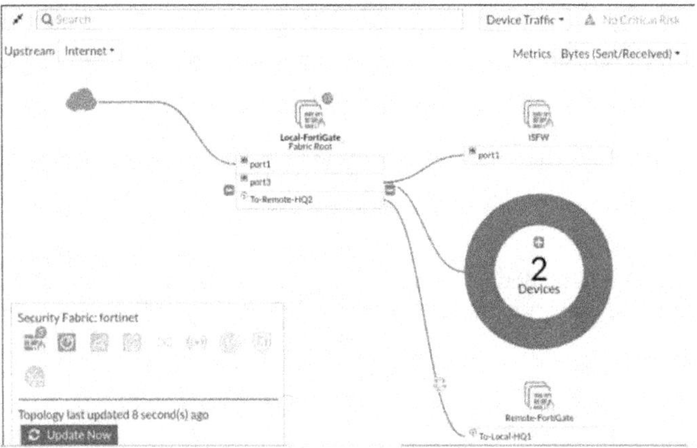

Given the security fabric topology shown in the exhibit, which two statements are true? (Choose two.)

A. There are five devices that are part of the security fabric.
B. Device detection is disabled on all FortiGate devices.
C. This security fabric topology is a logical topology view.
D. There are 19 security recommendations for the security fabric.

Answer: CD

References:

https://docs.fortinet.com/document/fortigate/5.6.0/cookbook/761085/results

https://docs.fortinet.com/document/fortimanager/6.2.0/new-features/736125/security-fabrictopology

Question: 19

A network administrator has enabled SSL certificate inspection and antivirus on FortiGate. When downloading an eICAR test file through HTTP, FortiGate detects the virus and blocks the file. When downloading the same file through HTTPS, FortiGate does not detect the virus and the file can be downloaded.

What is the reason for the failed virus detection by FortiGate?

A. The website is exempted from SSL inspection.
B. The eICAR test file exceeds the protocol options oversize limit.
C. The selected SSL inspection profile has certificate inspection enabled.
D. The browser does not trust the FortiGate self-signed CA certificate.

Answer: AD

https traffic requires SSL decryption. Check the ssh inspection profile

Question: 20

Refer to the exhibits.

Exhibit A | Exhibit B

```
# get system performance status
CPU states: 0% user 0% system 0% nice 100% idle 0% iowait 0% irq 0% softirq
CPU0 states: 0% user 0% system 0% nice 100% idle 0% iowait 0% irq 0% softirq
Memory: 2061108k total, 1854997k used (90%), 106111k free (5.1%), 100000k freeable (4.8%)
Average network usage: 83 / 0 kbps in 1 minute, 81 / 0 kbps in 10 minutes, 81 / 0 kbps in 30
minutes
Average sessions: 5 sessions in 1 minute, 3 sessions in 10 minutes, 3 sessions in 30 minutes
Average session setup rate: 0 sessions per second in last 1 minute, 0 sessions per second in last
10 minutes, 0 sessions per second in last 30 minutes
Virus caught: 0 total in 1 minute
IPS attacks blocked: 0 total in 1 minute
Uptime: 10 days,  3 hours,  28 minutes
```

Exhibit A | Exhibit B

```
config system global
    set memory-use-threshold-red 88
    set memory-use-threshold-extreme 95
    set memory-use-threshold-green 82
end
```

exhibit A shows system performance output. exhibit B shows a FortiGate configured with the default configuration of high memory usage thresholds. Based on the system performance output, which two statements are correct? (Choose two.)

A. Administrators can access FortiGate only through the console port.
B. FortiGate has entered conserve mode.
C. FortiGate will start sending all files to FortiSandbox for inspection.
D. Administrators cannot change the configuration.

Answer: BD

Reference: https://community.fortinet.com/t5/FortiGate/Technical-Tip-Conserve-mode-changes/tap/198502

https://community.fortinet.com/t5/FortiGate/Technical-Tip-Conserve-mode-changes/ta-p/198502

Though it is recommended to keep the default memory threshold, a new CLI command has been added to allow administrators to adjust the thresholds.

Default values are :

- red : 88% of total memory is considered "used memory"

- extreme : 95% of total memory is considered "used memory"

- green : 82% of total memory is considered "used memory"

Question: 21

Refer to the exhibits.

exhibit A.

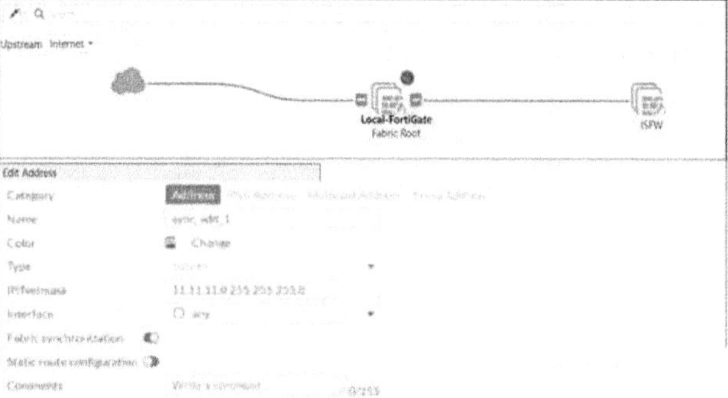

exhibit B.

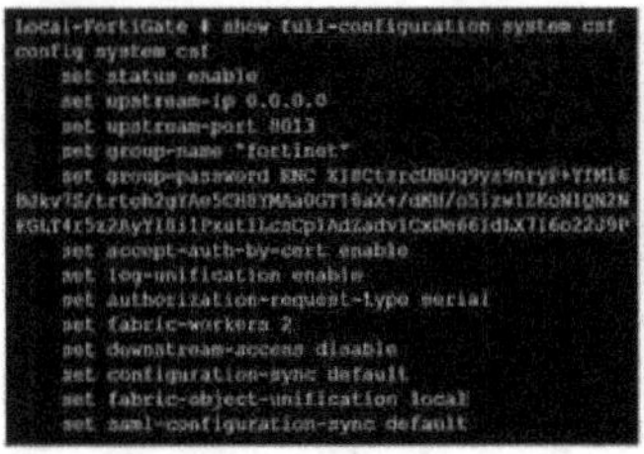

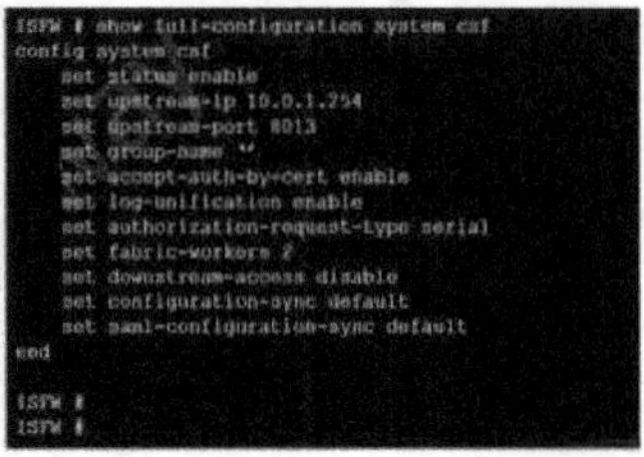

```
Local-FortiGate # show full-configuration system csf
config system csf
    set status enable
    set upstream-ip 0.0.0.0
    set upstream-port 8013
    set group-name "fortinet"
    set group-password ENC XI8CtzrcUBUq9yz9nryP+YIM16
BJkv7S/trtoh2gYAe5CH8YMAa0GT16aX+/dKH/o5IzwIZKoN1QN2N
EGLT4r5z2AyYI8i1PxutILcsCp1AdZadv1CxDe66IdLX7I6o22J9P
    set accept-auth-by-cert enable
    set log-unification enable
    set authorization-request-type serial
    set fabric-workers 2
    set downstream-access disable
    set configuration-sync default
    set fabric-object-unification local
    set saml-configuration-sync default
```

```
ISFW # show full-configuration system csf
config system csf
    set status enable
    set upstream-ip 10.0.1.254
    set upstream-port 8013
    set group-name ''
    set accept-auth-by-cert enable
    set log-unification enable
    set authorization-request-type serial
    set fabric-workers 2
    set downstream-access disable
    set configuration-sync default
    set saml-configuration-sync default
end

ISFW #
ISFW #
```

An administrator creates a new address object on the root FortiGate (Local-FortiGate) in the security fabric. After synchronization, this object is not available on the downstream FortiGate (ISFW).

What must the administrator do to synchronize the address object?

A. Change the csf setting on Local-FortiGate (root) to set configuration-sync local.
B. Change the csf setting on ISFW (downstream) to set configuration-sync local.
C. Change the csf setting on Local-FortiGate (root) to set fabric-object-unification default.
D. Change the csf setting on ISFW (downstream) to set fabric-object-unification default.

Answer: C

Reference:
https://docs.fortinet.com/document/fortigate/6.4.5/administrationguide/880913/synchronizing-objects-across-the-security-fabric

Question: 22

Which two settings can be separately configured per VDOM on a FortiGate device? (Choose two.)

A. System time

B. FortiGuaid update servers
C. Operating mode
D. NGFW mode

Answer: CD

C: "Operating mode is per-VDOM setting. You can combine transparent mode VDOM's with NAT mode VDOMs on the same physical Fortigate.

D: "Inspection-mode selection has moved from VDOM to firewall policy, and the default inspection mode is flow, so NGFW Mode can be changed from Profile-base (Default) to Policy-base directly in System > Settings from the VDOM" Page 125 of FortiGate_Infrastructure_6.4_Study_Guide

Question: 23

Which statement is correct regarding the inspection of some of the services available by web

applications embedded in third-party websites?

A. The security actions applied on the web applications will also be explicitly applied on the third-party websites.
B. The application signature database inspects traffic only from the original web application server.
C. FortiGuard maintains only one signature of each web application that is unique.
D. FortiGate can inspect sub-application traffic regardless where it was originated.

Answer: D

Reference:

https://help.fortinet.com/fortiproxy/11/Content/Admin%20Guides/FPXAdminGuide/300_System/303d_FortiG

Question: 24

An administrator wants to configure Dead Peer Detection (DPD) on IPSeC VPN for detecting dead tunnels. The requirement is that FortiGate sends DPD probes only when no traffic is observed in the tunnel.

Which DPD mode on FortiGate will meet the above requirement?

A. Disabled
B. On Demand
C. enabled
D. On Idle

Answer: D

Reference:
https://kb.fortinet.com/kb/documentLink.do?externalID=FD40813

Question: 25

Refer to the exhibit.

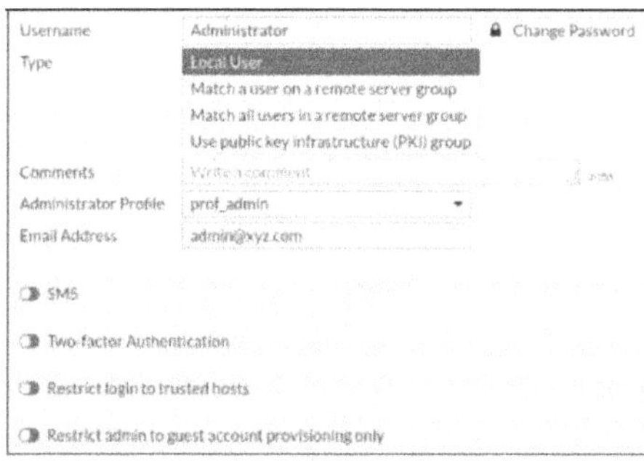

The global settings on a FortiGate device must be changed to align with company security policies.

What does the Administrator account need to access the FortiGate global settings?

A. Change password
B. enable restrict access to trusted hosts
C. Change Administrator profile
D. enable two-factor authentication

Answer: C

Reference:
https://kb.fortinet.com/kb/documentLink.do?externalID=FD34502

Question: 26

Which two statements are correct about SLA targets? (Choose two.)

A. You can configure only two SLA targets per one Performance SLA.
B. SLA targets are optional.

C. SLA targets are required for SD-WAN rules with a Best Quality strategy.
D. SLA targets are used only when referenced by an SD-WAN rule.

Answer: BD

Reference:
https://docs.fortinet.com/document/fortigate/6.2.0/cookbook/382233/performance-slasla-targets

Question: 27

Refer to the exhibit.

```
FGT1 # get router info routing-table database
Codes: K - kernel, C - connected, S - static, R - RIP, B - BGP
       O - OSPF, IA - OSPF inter area
       N1 - OSPF NSSA external type 1, N2 - OSPF NSSA external type 2
       E1 - OSPF external type 1, E2 - OSPF external type 2
       i - IS-IS, L1 - IS-IS level-1, L2 - IS-IS level-2, ia - IS-IS inter area
       > - selected route, * - FIB route, p - stale info

S      *> 0.0.0.0/0 [10/0] via 172.20.121.2, port1, [20/0]
       *>           [10/0] via 10.0.0.2, port2, [30/0]
S         0.0.0.0/0 [20/0] via 192.168.15.2, port3, [10/0]
C      *> 10.0.0.0/24 is directly connected, port2
S         172.13.24.0/24 [10.0] is directly connected, port4
C      *> 172.20.121.0/24 is directly connected, port1
S      *> 192.167.1.0/24 [10/0] via 10.0.0.2, port2
C      *> 192.168.15.0/24 is directly connected, port3
```

Given the routing database shown in the exhibit, which two statements are correct? (Choose two.)

A. The port3 default route has the highest distance.
B. The port3 default route has the lowest metric.
C. There will be eight routes active in the routing table.
D. The port1 and port2 default routes are active in the routing table.

Answer: AD

Question: 28

When configuring a firewall virtual wire pair policy, which following statement is true?

A. Any number of virtual wire pairs can be included, as long as the policy traffic direction is the same.
B. Only a single virtual wire pair can be included in each policy.
C. Any number of virtual wire pairs can be included in each policy, regardless of the policy traffic direction settings.
D. exactly two virtual wire pairs need to be included in each policy.

Answer: A

Reference:
https://kb.fortinet.com/kb/documentLink.do?externalID=FD48690

Question: 29

Refer to the exhibit.

```
Fortigate # diagnose sniffer packet any "icmp" 5
interfaces=[any]
filters=[icmp]
20.370482 port2 in 10.0.1.2 -> 8.8.8.8: icmp: echo request
0x0000   4500 003c 2f8f 0000 8001 f020 0a00 0102        E..</...........
0x0010   0808 0808 0800 4d5a 0001 0001 6162 6364        ......MZ....abcd
0x0020   6566 6768 696a 6b6c 6d6e 6f70 7172 7374        efghijklmnopqrst
0x0030   7576 7761 6263 6465 6667 6869                  uvwabcdefghi

20.370805 port1 out 10.56.240.228 -> 8.8.8.8: icmp: echo request
0x0000   4500 003c 2f8f 0000 7f01 0106 0a38 f0e4        E..</........8..
0x0010   0808 0808 0800 6159 ec01 0001 6162 6364        ......aY....abcd
0x0020   6566 6768 696a 6b6c 6d6e 6f70 7172 7374        efghijklmnopqrst
0x0030   7576 7761 6263 6465 6667 6869                  uvwabcdefghi

20.372138 port1 in 8.8.8.8 -> 10.56.240.228: icmp: echo reply
0x0000   4500 003c 0000 0000 7501 3a95 0808 0808        E..<....u.:.....
0x0010   0a38 f0e4 0000 6959 ec01 0001 6162 6364        .8....iY....abcd
0x0020   6566 6768 696a 6b6c 6d6e 6f70 7172 7374        efghijklmnopqrst
0x0030   7576 7761 6263 6465 6667 6869                  uvwabcdefghi

20.372163 port2 out 8.8.8.8 -> 10.0.1.2: icmp: echo reply
0x0000   4500 003c 0000 0000 7401 2bb0 0808 0808        E..<....t.+.....
0x0010   0a00 0102 0000 555a 0001 0001 6162 6364        ......UZ....abcd
0x0020   6566 6768 696a 6b6c 6d6e 6f70 7172 7374        efghijklmnopqrst
0x0030   7576 7761 6263 6465 6667 6869                  uvwabcdefghi
```

An administrator is running a sniffer command as shown in the exhibit.

Which three pieces of information are included in the sniffer output? (Choose three.)

A. Interface name
B. ethernet header
C. IP header
D. Application header
E. Packet payload

Answer: ACe

Reference:
https://kb.fortinet.com/kb/documentLink.do?externalID=11186

Study Guide – Routing – Diagnostics – Packet Capture Verbosity Level.

diagnose sniffer packet <interface> '<filter>' <verbosity> <count> <timestamp> <frame size>

In the example, verbosity is 5.

The verbosity level specifies how much info you want to display.

1 (default): IP Headers.

2: IP Headers, Packet Payload.

3. IP Headers, Packet Payload, ethernet Headers.

4: IP Headers, Interface Name.

5: IP Headers, Packet Payload, Interface Name.

6: IP Headers, Packet Payload, ethernet Headers, Interface Name.

Question: 30

An administrator does not want to report the logon events of service accounts to FortiGate. What

setting on the collector agent is required to achieve this?

A. Add the support of NTLM authentication.
B. Add user accounts to Active Directory (AD).
C. Add user accounts to the FortiGate group fitter.
D. Add user accounts to the Ignore User List.

Answer: D

Reference: https://community.fortinet.com/t5/Support-Forum/Collector-Agent-and-problemgetting-login-info/m-p/95481

Question: 31

An administrator is configuring an IPsec VPN between site A and site B. The Remote Gateway setting in both sites has been configured as

Static IP Address. For site A, the local quick mode selector is 192. 168. 1.0/24 and the remote quick mode selector is 192. 168.2.0/24.

Which subnet must the administrator configure for the local quick mode selector for site B?

A. 192. 168. 1.0/24
B. 192. 168.0.0/24
C. 192. 168.2.0/24
D. 192. 168.3.0/24

Answer: C

Question: 32

Which two statements are true about the FGCP protocol? (Choose two.)

A. FGCP elects the primary FortiGate device.
B. FGCP is not used when FortiGate is in transparent mode.
C. FGCP runs only over the heartbeat links.
D. FGCP is used to discover FortiGate devices in different HA groups.

Answer: AC

Reference:

https://docs.fortinet.com/document/fortigate/6.4.0/ports-and-protocols/564712/fgcp-fortigateclustering-protocol

Question: 33

Which two attributes are required on a certificate so it can be used as a CA certificate on SSL Inspection? (Choose two.)

A. The keyUsage extension must be set to keyCertSign.
B. The common name on the subject field must use a wildcard name.
C. The issuer must be a public CA.
D. The CA extension must be set to TRUe.

Answer: AD

"In order for FortiGate to act in these roles, its CA certificate must have the basic constraints extension set to cA=True and the value of the keyUsage extension set to keyCertSign."

Reference:
https://www.reddit.com/r/fortinet/comments/c7j6jg/recommended_ssl_cert/

Question: 34

Which two inspection modes can you use to configure a firewall policy on a profile-based nextgeneration firewall (NGFW)? (Choose two.)

A. Proxy-based inspection
B. Certificate inspection
C. Flow-based inspection
D. Full Content inspection

Answer: AC

Question: 35

Refer to the exhibit.

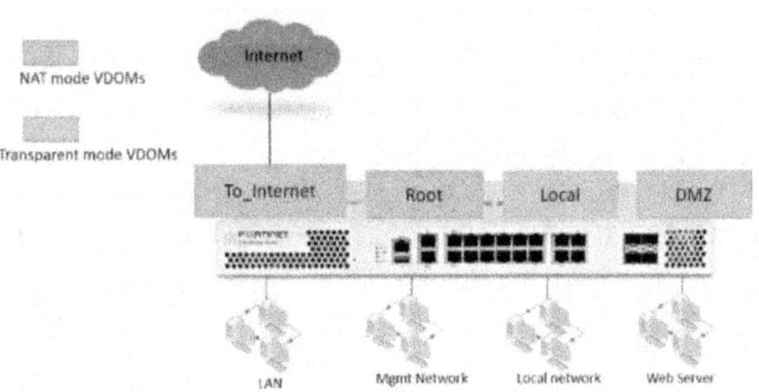

The Root and To_Internet VDOMs are configured in NAT mode. The DMZ and Local VDOMs are configured in transparent mode.

The Root VDOM is the management VDOM. The To_Internet VDOM allows LAN users to access the internet. The To_Internet VDOM is the only VDOM with internet access and is directly connected to ISP modem .

With this configuration, which statement is true?

A. Inter-VDOM links are required to allow traffic between the Local and Root VDOMs.
B. A static route is required on the To_Internet VDOM to allow LAN users to access the internet.
C. Inter-VDOM links are required to allow traffic between the Local and DMZ VDOMs.
D. Inter-VDOM links are not required between the Root and To_Internet VDOMs because the Root

VDOM is used only as a management VDOM.

Answer: A

Reference:
https://kb.fortinet.com/kb/documentLink.do?externalID=FD46542

Question: 36

Refer to the exhibit.

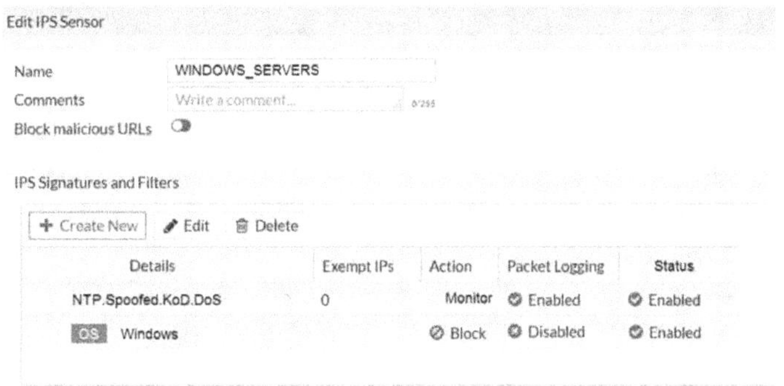

The exhibit shows the IPS sensor configuration.

If traffic matches this IPS sensor, which two actions is the sensor expected to take? (Choose two.)

A. The sensor will allow attackers matching the Microsoft Windows.iSCSI.Target.DoS signature.
B. The sensor will block all attacks aimed at Windows servers.
C. The sensor will reset all connections that match these signatures.
D. The sensor will gather a packet log for all matched traffic.

Answer: AB

Question: 37

Which CLI command allows administrators to troubleshoot Layer 2 issues, such as an IP address conflict?

A. get system status
B. get system performance status
C. diagnose sys top
D. get system arp

Answer: D

"If you suspect that there is an IP address conflict, or that an IP has been assigned to the wrong

device, you may need to look at the ARP table."

Question: 38

Refer to the exhibit showing a debug flow output.

```
id=20085 trace_id=1 func=print_pkt_detail line=5594 msg="vd-root:0 received a packet(proto=1,
10.0.1.10:19938->10.0.1.250:2048) from port1. type=8, code=0, id=19938, seq=1."
id=20085 trace_id=1 func=init_ip_session_common line=5760 msg="allocate a new session-00003dd5"
id=20085 trace_id=1 func=vf_ip_route_input_common line=2598 msg="find a route: flag=84000000 gw-
10.0.1.250 via root"
id=20085 trace_id=2 func=print_pkt_detail line=5594 msg="vd-root:0 received a packet(proto=1,
10.0.1.250:19938->10.0.1.10:0) from local. type=0, code=0, id=19938, seq=1."
id=20085 trace_id=2 func=resolve_ip_tuple_fast line=5675 msg="Find an existing session, id-
00003dd5, reply direction"
```

Which two statements about the debug flow output are correct? (Choose two.)

A. The debug flow is of ICMP traffic.
B. A firewall policy allowed the connection.
C. A new traffic session is created.
D. The default route is required to receive a reply.

Answer: AC

Reference:
https://docs.fortinet.com/document/fortigate/6.2.3/cookbook/54688/debugging-thepacket-flow

Question: 39

Which two settings are required for SSL VPN to function between two FortiGate devices? (Choose two.)

A. The client FortiGate requires a client certificate signed by the CA on the server FortiGate.
B. The client FortiGate requires a manually added route to remote subnets.
C. The client FortiGate uses the SSL VPN tunnel interface type to connect SSL VPN.
D. The server FortiGate requires a CA certificate to verify the client FortiGate certificate.

Answer: CD

https://docs.fortinet.com/document/fortigate/7.0.9/administration-guide/508779/fortigate-as-sslvpn-client

Question: 40

On FortiGate, which type of logs record information about traffic directly to and from the FortiGate

management IP addresses?

A. System event logs
B. Forward traffic logs

C. Local traffic logs
D. Security logs

Answer: C

Reference:
https://docs.fortinet.com/document/fortigate/5.4.0/cookbook/47697
0

Traffic logs record the traffic flowing through your FortiGate unit. Since traffic needs firewall policies to properly flow through FortiGate, this type of logging is also called firewall policy logging. Firewall policies control all traffic attempting to pass through the FortiGate unit, between FortiGate interfaces, zones, and VLAN sub-interfaces.

Question: 41

Which statement about the policy ID number of a firewall policy is true?

A. It is required to modify a firewall policy using the CLI.
B. It represents the number of objects used in the firewall policy.
C. It changes when firewall policies are reordered.
D. It defines the order in which rules are processed.

Answer: A

Question: 42

Refer to the exhibits.

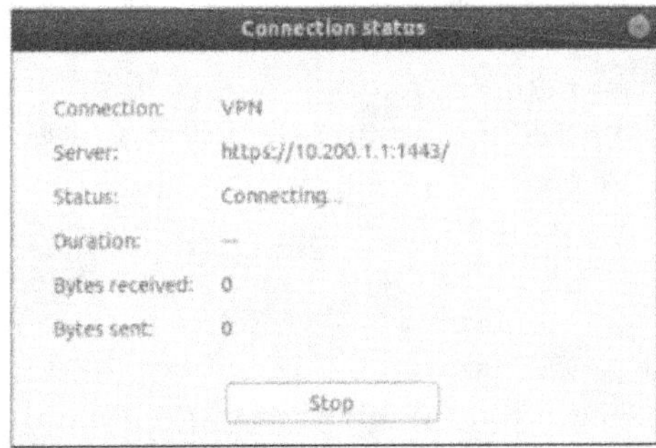

The SSL VPN connection fails when a user attempts to connect to it. What should the user do to successfully connect to SSL VPN?

A. Change the SSL VPN port on the client.
B. Change the Server IP address.

C. Change the idle-timeout.
D. Change the SSL VPN portal to the tunnel.

Answer: A

Reference:
https://docs.fortinet.com/document/fortigate/5.4.0/cookbook/15049
4

Question: 43

An administrator has configured a strict RPF check on FortiGate. Which statement is true about the strict RPF check?

A. The strict RPF check is run on the first sent and reply packet of any new session.
B. Strict RPF checks the best route back to the source using the incoming interface.
C. Strict RPF checks only for the existence of at least one active route back to the source using the incoming interface.
D. Strict RPF allows packets back to sources with all active routes.

Answer: C

Reference: https://community.fortinet.com/t5/FortiGate/Technical-Note-Reverse-Path-ForwardingRPF-implementation-and/ta-p/194382

Reference:
https://kb.fortinet.com/kb/documentLink.do?externalID=FD33955

Question: 44

Refer to the exhibits.

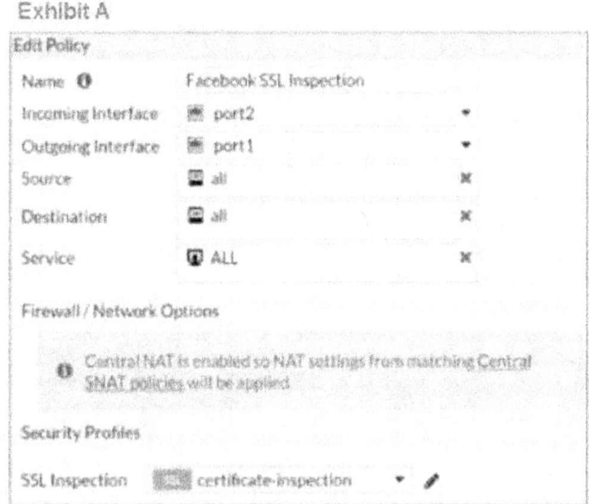

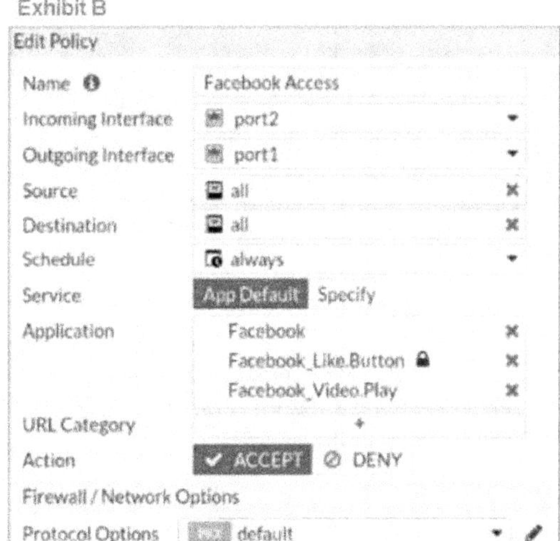

The exhibits show the SSL and authentication policy (exhibit A) and the security policy (exhibit B) for Facebook .

Users are given access to the Facebook web application. They can play video content hosted on Facebook but they are unable to leave reactions on videos or other types of posts.

Which part of the policy configuration must you change to resolve the issue?

A. Make SSL inspection needs to be a deep content inspection.
B. Force access to Facebook using the HTTP service.
C. Get the additional application signatures are required to add to the security policy.
D. Add Facebook in the URL category in the security policy.

Answer: A

The lock logo behind Facebook_like.Button indicates that SSL Deep Inspection is Required.

Question: 45

Which two statements about FortiGate FSSO agentless polling mode are true? (Choose two.)

A. FortiGate uses the AD server as the collector agent.
B. FortiGate uses the SMB protocol to read the event viewer logs from the DCs.
C. FortiGate does not support workstation check .
D. FortiGate directs the collector agent to use a remote LDAP server.

Answer: BC

You can deploy FSSO w/o installing an agent. FG polls the DCs directly, instead of receiving logon info indirectly from a collector agent.

Because FG collects all of the data itself, agentless polling mode requires greater system resources, and it doesn't scale as easily.

Agentless polling mode operates in a similar way to WinSecLog, but with only two event IDs: 4768 and 4769. Because there's no collector agent, FG uses the SMB protocol to read the event viewer logs from the DCs.

FG acts as a collector. It 's responsible for polling on top of its normal FSSO tasks but does not have all the extra features, such as workstation checks, that are available with the external collector agent.

Reference:
https://kb.fortinet.com/kb/documentLink.do?externalID=FD47732

https://community.fortinet.com/t5/FortiGate/Troubleshooting-Tip-How-to-troubleshoot-FSSOagentless-polling/ta-p/214349

Question: 46

Refer to the exhibit.

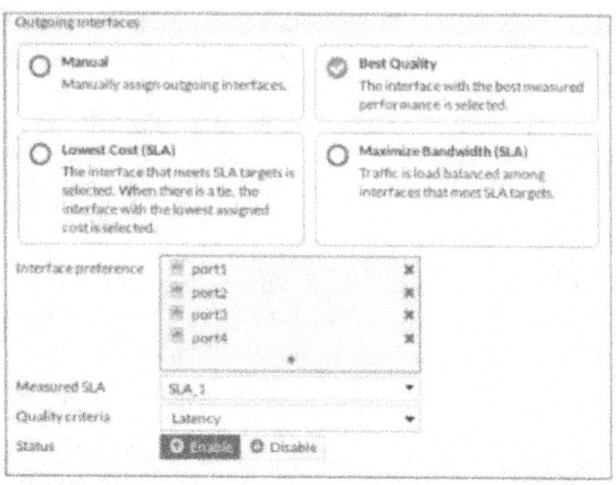

The exhibit contains the configuration for an SD-WAN Performance SLA, as well as the output of diagnose sys virtual-wan-link health-check . Which interface will be selected as an outgoing interface?

A. port2
B. port4
C. port3
D. port1

Answer: D

Port 1 shows the lowest latency.

Question: 47

Refer to the exhibit.

Review the Intrusion Prevention System (IPS) profile signature settings. Which statement is correct in adding the FTP.Login.Failed signature to the IPS sensor profile?

A. The signature setting uses a custom rating threshold.
B. The signature setting includes a group of other signatures.
C. Traffic matching the signature will be allowed and logged.
D. Traffic matching the signature will be silently dropped and logged.

Answer: D

Action is drop, signature default action is listed only in the signature, it would only match if action was set to default.

Question: 48

Refer to the exhibit.

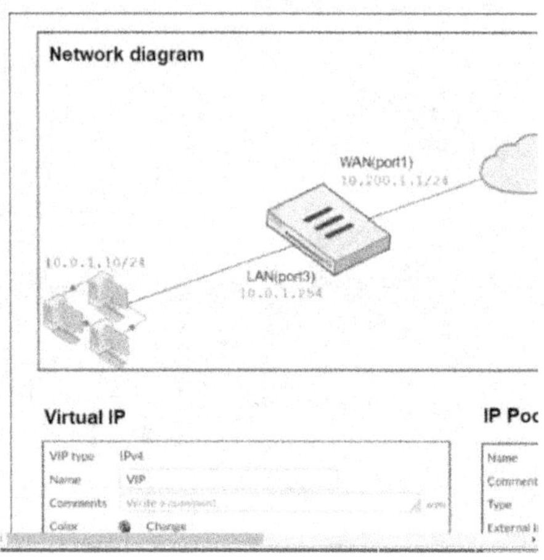

The exhibit contains a network diagram, virtual IP, IP pool, and firewall policies configuration.

The WAN (port1) interface has the IP address 10.200. 1. 1/24.

The LAN (port3) interface has the IP address 10 .0.1.254. /24.

The first firewall policy has NAT enabled using IP Pool.

The second firewall policy is configured with a VIP as the destination address.

Which IP address will be used to source NAT the internet traffic coming from a workstation with the IP address 10.0. 1. 10?

A. 10.200. 1. 1
B. 10.200.3. 1
C. 10.200. 1. 100
D. 10.200. 1. 10

Answer: C

Policy 1 is applied on outbound (LAN-WAN) and policy 2 is applied on inbound (WAN-LAN). Question is asking SNAT for outbound traffic so policy 1 will take place and NAT overload is in effect.

Question: 49

Refer to the exhibit.

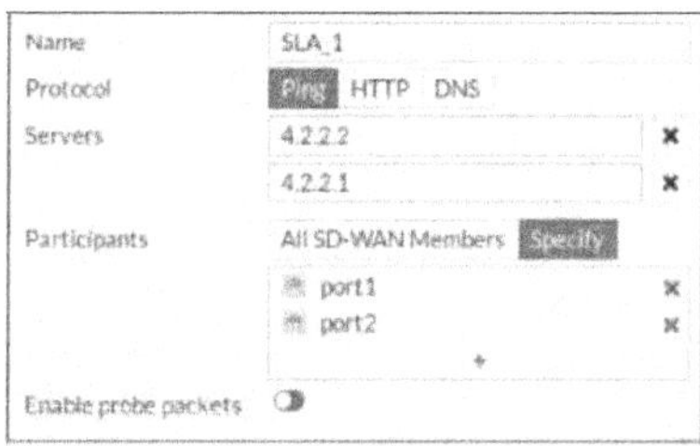

An administrator has configured a performance SLA on FortiGate, which failed to generate any traffic.

Why is FortiGate not sending probes to 4.2.2.2 and 4.2.2.1 servers? (Choose two.)

A. The Detection Mode setting is not set to Passive.
B. Administrator didn't configure a gateway for the SD-WAN members, or configured gateway is not valid.
C. The configured participants are not SD-WAN members.
D. The enable probe packets setting is not enabled.

Answer: BD

Question: 50

Refer to the exhibit.

```
STUDENT # get system session list
PROTO   EXPIRE SOURCE            SOURCE-NAT          DESTINATION          DESTINATION-NAT
tcp     3598   10.0.1.10:2706    10.200.1.6:2706     10.200.1.254:80      -
tcp     3598   10.0.1.10:2704    10.200.1.6:2704     10.200.1.254:80      -
tcp     3596   10.0.1.10:2702    10.200.1.6:2702     10.200.1.254:80      -
tcp     3599   10.0.1.10:2700    10.200.1.6:2700     10.200.1.254:443     -
tcp     3599   10.0.1.10:2698    10.200.1.6:2698     10.200.1.254:80      -
tcp     3598   10.0.1.10:2696    10.200.1.6:2696     10.200.1.254:443     -
udp     174    10.0.1.10:2694    -                     10.0.1.254:53      -
udp     173    10.0.1.10:2690    -                     10.0.1.254:53      -
```

Which contains a session list output. Based on the information shown in the exhibit, which statement is true?

A. Destination NAT is disabled in the firewall policy.
B. One-to-one NAT IP pool is used in the firewall policy.
C. Overload NAT IP pool is used in the firewall policy.
D. Port block allocation IP pool is used in the firewall policy.

Answer: B

FortiGate_Security_6.4 page 155 . In one-to-one, PAT is not required.

Question: 51

FortiGuard categories can be overridden and defined in different categories. To create a web rating override for example.com home page, the override must be configured using a specific syntax.

Which two syntaxes are correct to configure web rating for the home page? (Choose two.)

A. www.example.com:443
B. www.example.com
C. example.com

D. www.example.com/index.html

Answer: BC

When using FortiGuard category filtering to allow or block access to a website, one option is to make a web rating override and define the website in a different category. Web ratings are only for host names - no URLs or wildcard characters are allowed.

OK: google.com or www.google.com

NO OK: www.google.com/index.html or google.*

FortiGate_Security_6.4 page 384

When using FortiGuard category filtering to allow or block access to a website, one option is to make a web rating override and define the website in a different category. Web ratings are only for host names-- "no URLs or wildcard characters are allowed".

Question: 52

Refer to the exhibit.

```
vcluster_nr=1
vcluster_0: start_time=1593701974(2020-07-02 10:59:34), state/o/chg_time=2(work)/2
(work)/1593701169(2020-07-02 10:46:09)
     pingsvr_flip_timeout/expire=3600s/2781s
     'FGVM010000064692': ha_prio/o=1/1, link_failure=0, pingsvr_failure=0, flag=
0x00000000, uptime/reset_cnt=198/0
     'FGVM010000065036': ha_prio/o=0/0, link_failure=0, pingsvr_failure=0, flag=
0x00000001, uptime/reset_cnt=0/1
```

The exhibit displays the output of the CLI command: diagnose sys ha dump-by vcluster.

Which two statements are true? (Choose two.)

A. FortiGate SN FGVM010000065036 HA uptime has been reset.
B. FortiGate devices are not in sync because one device is down.
C. FortiGate SN FGVM010000064692 is the primary because of higher HA uptime.
D. FortiGate SN FGVM010000064692 has the higher HA priority.

Answer: AD

1. Override is disable by default - OK

2. "If the HA uptime of a device is AT LeAST FIVe MINUTeS (300 seconds) MORe than the HA Uptime of the other FortiGate devices, it becomes the primary,

https://docs.fortinet.com/document/fortigate/6.0.0/handbook/666653/primary-unit-selection-withoverride-disab

Question: 53

Which three authentication timeout types are availability for selection on FortiGate? (Choose three.)

A. hard-timeout
B. auth-on-demand
C. soft-timeout
D. new-session
E. Idle-timeout

Answer: ADe

https://kb.fortinet.com/kb/documentLink.do?externalID=FD37221

Question: 54

Refer to the exhibit.

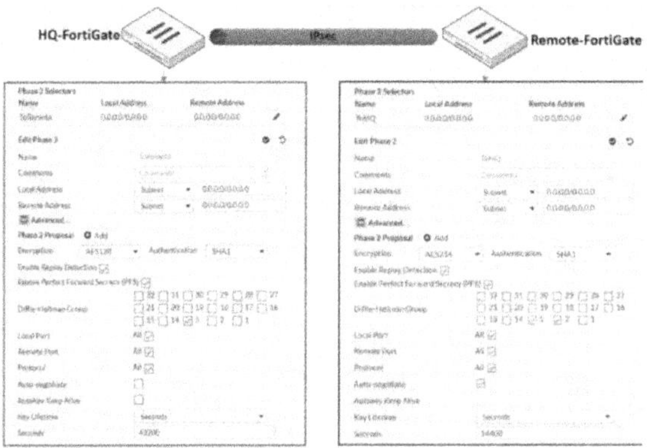

A network administrator is troubleshooting an IPsec tunnel between two FortiGate devices. The administrator has determined that phase 1 status is up. but phase 2 fails to come up.

Based on the phase 2 configuration shown in the exhibit, what configuration change will bring phase 2 up?

A. On HQ-FortiGate, enable Auto-negotiate.
B. On Remote-FortiGate, set Seconds to 43200.
C. On HQ-FortiGate, enable Diffie-Hellman Group 2.
D. On HQ-FortiGate, set encryption to AeS256.

Answer: D

Reference:
https://docs.fortinet.com/document/fortigate/5.4.0/cookbook/168495

encryption and authentication algorithm needs to match in order for IPSeC be successfully established.

Question: 55

Which three options are the remote log storage options you can configure on FortiGate? (Choose three.)

A. FortiCache
B. FortiSIeM
C. FortiAnalyzer
D. FortiSandbox
E. FortiCloud

Answer: BCe

Reference:

https://docs.fortinet.com/document/fortigate/6.0.0/handbook/265052/logging-and-reportingoverview

Question: 56

A network administrator is configuring a new IPsec VPN tunnel on FortiGate. The remote peer IP address is dynamic. In addition, the remote peer does not support a dynamic DNS update service.

What type of remote gateway should the administrator configure on FortiGate for the new IPsec VPN tunnel to work?

A. Static IP Address
B. Dialup User
C. Dynamic DNS
D. Pre-shared Key

Answer: B

Dialup user is used when the remote peer's IP address is unknown. The remote peer whose IP address is unknown acts as the dialup clien and this is often the case for branch offices and mobile

VPN clients that use dynamic IP address and no dynamic DNS

Question: 57

An administrator has configured outgoing Interface any in a firewall policy. Which statement is true about the policy list view?

A. Policy lookup will be disabled.
B. By Sequence view will be disabled.
C. Search option will be disabled
D. Interface Pair view will be disabled.

Answer: D

https://kb.fortinet.com/kb/documentLink.do?externalID=FD47821

Question: 58

Which statement correctly describes NetAPI polling mode for the FSSO collector agent?

A. The collector agent uses a Windows API to query DCs for user logins.
B. NetAPI polling can increase bandwidth usage in large networks.
C. The collector agent must search security event logs.
D. The NetSession enum function is used to track user logouts.

Answer: D

FortiGate_Infrastructure_7.0 page 270: "NetAPI: polls temporary sessions created on the DC when a user logs in or logs out and calls the NetSessionenum function in Windows."

Reference:
https://kb.fortinet.com/kb/documentLink.do?externalID=FD34906

https://kb.fortinet.com/kb/microsites/search.do?cmd=displayKC&docType=kc&externalId=FD34906&sliceId=1

Question: 59

An administrator has configured the following settings:

```
config system settings
set ses-denied-traffic enable
end
config system global
set block-session-timer 30
end
```

What are the two results of this configuration? (Choose two.)

A. Device detection on all interfaces is enforced for 30 minutes.
B. Denied users are blocked for 30 minutes.
C. A session for denied traffic is created.
D. The number of logs generated by denied traffic is reduced.

Answer: CD

ses-denied-traffic

enable/disable including denied session in the session table.

https://docs.fortinet.com/document/fortigate/7.0.6/cli-reference/20620/config-system-settings

block-session-timer

Duration in seconds for blocked sessions .

integer

Minimum value: 1 Maximum value: 300

30

https://docs.fortinet.com/document/fortigate/7.0.6/cli-reference/1620/config-system-global

Reference:
https://kb.fortinet.com/kb/documentLink.do?externalID=FD46328

Question: 60

In an explicit proxy setup, where is the authentication method and database configured?

A. Proxy Policy
B. Authentication Rule
C. Firewall Policy
D. Authentication scheme

Answer: D

Question: 61

In consolidated firewall policies, IPv4 and IPv6 policies are combined in a single consolidated policy.

Instead of separate policies. Which three statements are true about consolidated IPv4 and IPv6 policy configuration? (Choose three.)

A. The IP version of the sources and destinations in a firewall policy must be different.
B. The Incoming Interface. Outgoing Interface. Schedule, and Service fields can be shared with both IPv4 and IPv6.
C. The policy table in the GUI can be filtered to display policies with IPv4, IPv6 or IPv4 and IPv6 sources and destinations.
D. The IP version of the sources and destinations in a policy must match.
E. The policy table in the GUI will be consolidated to display policies with IPv4 and IPv6 sources and destinations.

Answer: BDe

Question: 62

Which of the following are valid actions for FortiGuard category based filter in a web filter profile ui proxy-based inspection mode? (Choose two.)

A. Warning
B. exempt
C. Allow
D. Learn

Answer: AC

Question: 63

examine this FortiGate configuration:

```
config authentication setting
     set active-auth-scheme SCHEME1
end
config authentication rule
     edit WebProxyRule
       set srcaddr 10.0.1.0/24
       set active-auth-method SCHEME2
     next
end
```

How does the FortiGate handle web proxy traffic coming from the IP address 10.2.1.200 that requires authorization?

A. It always authorizes the traffic without requiring authentication.
B. It drops the traffic.
C. It authenticates the traffic using the authentication scheme SCHeMe2.
D. It authenticates the traffic using the authentication scheme SCHeMe1.

Answer: D

"What happens to traffic that requires authorization, but does not match any authentication rule?

The active and passive SSO schemes to use for those cases is defined under config authentication setting"

Question: 64

Which two types of traffic are managed only by the management VDOM? (Choose two.)

A. FortiGuard web filter queries
B. PKI
C. Traffic shaping
D. DNS

Answer: AD

Question: 65

Refer to the exhibit.

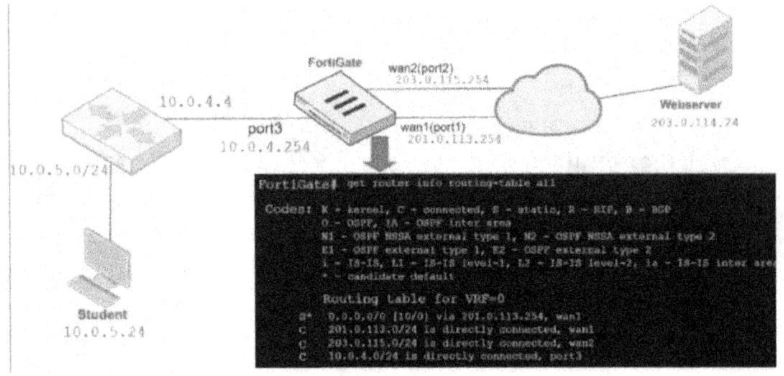

Which contains a network diagram and routing table output.

The Student is unable to access Webserver.

What is the cause of the problem and what is the solution for the problem?

A. The first packet sent from Student failed the RPF check.
B. This issue can be resolved by adding a static route to 10.0.4.0/24 through wan1.

C. The first reply packet for Student failed the RPF check.
D. This issue can be resolved by adding a static route to 10.0.4.0/24 through wan1.
E. The first reply packet for Student failed the RPF check .
F. This issue can be resolved by adding a static route to 203.0. 114.24/32 through port3.
G. The first packet sent from Student failed the RPF check.
H. This issue can be resolved by adding a static route to 203.0. 114.24/32 through port3.

Answer: D

Question: 66

Which CLI command will display sessions both from client to the proxy and from the proxy to the servers?

A. diagnose wad session list
B. diagnose wad session list | grep hook-pre&&hook-out
C. diagnose wad session list | grep hook=pre&&hook=out
D. diagnose wad session list | grep "hook=pre"&"hook=out"

Answer: A

Question: 67

Which three criteria can a FortiGate use to look for a matching firewall policy to process traffic?

(Choose three.)

A. Source defined as Internet Services in the firewall policy.
B. Destination defined as Internet Services in the firewall policy.
C. Highest to lowest priority defined in the firewall policy.

D. Services defined in the firewall policy.
E. Lowest to highest policy ID number.

Answer: ABD

When a packet arrives, how does FortiGate find a matching policy? each policy has match criteria, which you can define using the following objects:

• Incoming Interface

• Outgoing Interface

• Source: IP address, user, internet services

• Destination: IP address or internet services

• Service: IP protocol and port number

• Schedule: Applies during configured times

Reference:
https://kb.fortinet.com/kb/documentLink.do?externalID=FD47435

Question: 68

Which scanning technique on FortiGate can be enabled only on the CLI?

A. Heuristics scan
B. Trojan scan
C. Antivirus scan
D. Ransomware scan

Answer: A

Reference:
https://docs.fortinet.com/document/fortigate/6.0.0/handbook/567568/enablingscanning

Question: 69

Refer to the exhibit to view the application control profile.

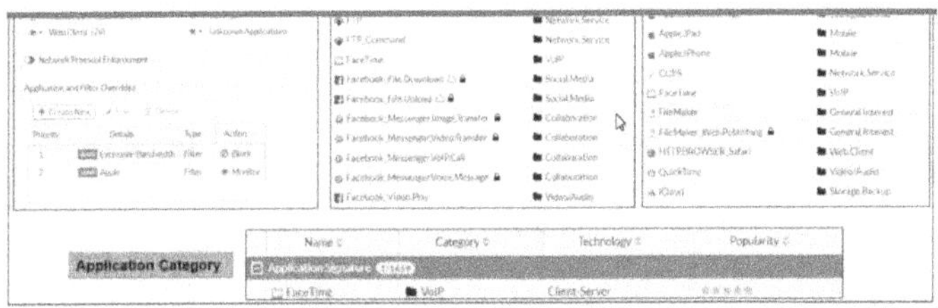

Based on the configuration, what will happen to Apple FaceTime?

A. Apple FaceTime will be blocked, based on the excessive-Bandwidth filter configuration
B. Apple FaceTime will be allowed, based on the Apple filter configuration.
C. Apple FaceTime will be allowed only if the filter in Application and Filter Overrides is set to Learn
D. Apple FaceTime will be allowed, based on the Categories configuration.

Answer: A

Question: 70

An administrator must disable RPF check to investigate an issue.

Which method is best suited to disable RPF without affecting features like antivirus and intrusion prevention system?

A. enable asymmetric routing, so the RPF check will be bypassed.
B. Disable the RPF check at the FortiGate interface level for the source check.
C. Disable the RPF check at the FortiGate interface level for the reply check .
D. enable asymmetric routing at the interface level.

Answer: B

eference:
https://kb.fortinet.com/kb/documentLink.do?externalID=FD33955

Question: 71

An administrator is configuring an Ipsec between site A and siteB. The Remotes Gateway setting in both sites has been configured as Static IP Address. For site A, the local quick mode selector is 192. 16. 1.0/24 and the remote quick mode selector is 192. 16.2.0/24. How must the administrator configure the local quick mode selector for site B?

A. 192. 168.3.0/24
B. 192. 168.2.0/24
C. 192. 168. 1.0/24
D. 192. 168.0.0/8

Answer: B

Question: 72

Which of the following statements about central NAT are true? (Choose two.)

A. IP tool references must be removed from existing firewall policies before enabling central NAT .
B. Central NAT can be enabled or disabled from the CLI only.
C. Source NAT, using central NAT, requires at least one central SNAT policy.
D. Destination NAT, using central NAT, requires a VIP object as the destination address in a firewall.

Answer: AB

Quetion: 73

An organization's employee needs to connect to the office through a high-latency internet

connection.

Which SSL VPN setting should the administrator adjust to prevent the SSL VPN negotiation failure?

A. Change the session-ttl.
B. Change the login timeout.
C. Change the idle-timeout.
D. Change the udp idle timer.

Answer: B

Question: 74

An administrator observes that the port1 interface cannot be configured with an IP address. What can be the reasons for that? (Choose three.)

A. The interface has been configured for one-arm sniffer.
B. The interface is a member of a virtual wire pair.
C. The operation mode is transparent.
D. The interface is a member of a zone.
E. Captive portal is enabled in the interface.

Answer: ABC

https://help.fortinet.com/fos50hlp/54/Content/FortiOS/fortigate-whats-new54/Top_VirtualWirePair.htm

Question: 75

Which two statements are correct about a software switch on FortiGate? (Choose two.)

A. It can be configured only when FortiGate is operating in NAT mode
B. Can act as a Layer 2 switch as well as a Layer 3 router
C. All interfaces in the software switch share the same IP address
D. It can group only physical interfaces

Answer: AC

Question: 76

Which two statements are correct regarding FortiGate FSSO agentless polling mode? (Choose two.)

A. FortiGate points the collector agent to use a remote LDAP server.
B. FortiGate uses the AD server as the collector agent.
C. FortiGate uses the SMB protocol to read the event viewer logs from the DCs.
D. FortiGate queries AD by using the LDAP to retrieve user group information.

Answer: CD

Fortigate Infrastructure 7.0 Study Guide P.272-273

https://kb.fortinet.com/kb/documentLink.do?externalID=FD47732

Question: 77

What is the limitation of using a URL list and application control on the same firewall policy, in NGFW policy-based mode?

A. It limits the scope of application control to the browser-based technology category only.
B. It limits the scope of application control to scan application traffic based on application category only.
C. It limits the scope of application control to scan application traffic using parent signatures only
D. It limits the scope of application control to scan application traffic on DNS protocol only.

Answer: B

Question: 78

examine this output from a debug flow:

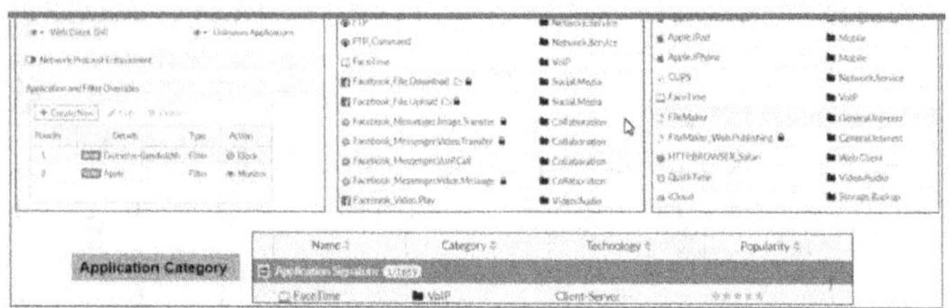

Why did the FortiGate drop the packet?

A. The next-hop IP address is unreachable.
B. It failed the RPF check .
C. It matched an explicitly configured firewall policy with the action DeNY.
D. It matched the default implicit firewall policy.

Answer: D

https://kb.fortinet.com/kb/documentLink.do?externalID=13900

Question: 79

Which three security features require the intrusion prevention system (IPS) engine to function? (Choose three.)

A. Web filter in flow-based inspection
B. Antivirus in flow-based inspection
C. DNS filter
D. Web application firewall
E. Application control

Answer: ABe

https://docs.fortinet.com/document/fortigate/7.0.0/new-features/739623/dns-filter-handled-byips-engine-in-flow-mode

Question: 80

Which of the following statements about backing up logs from the CLI and downloading logs from the GUI are true? (Choose two.)

A. Log downloads from the GUI are limited to the current filter view
B. Log backups from the CLI cannot be restored to another FortiGate.
C. Log backups from the CLI can be configured to upload to FTP as a scheduled time
D. Log downloads from the GUI are stored as LZ4 compressed files.

Answer: AB

Question: 81

An administrator needs to increase network bandwidth and provide redundancy.

What interface type must the administrator select to bind multiple FortiGate interfaces?

A. VLAN interface
B. Software Switch interface
C. Aggregate interface
D. Redundant interface

Answer: C

Reference: https://forum.fortinet.com/tm.aspx?m=120324

Question: 82

Refer to the exhibit.

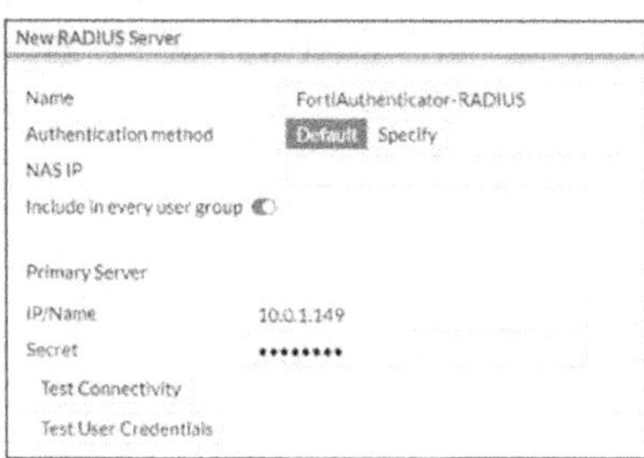

An administrator added a configuration for a new RADIUS server. While configuring, the administrator selected the Include in every user group option.

What is the impact of using the Include in every user group option in a RADIUS configuration?

A. This option places the RADIUS server, and all users who can authenticate against that server, into every FortiGate user group.
B. This option places all FortiGate users and groups required to authenticate into the RADIUS server, which, in this case, is FortiAuthenticator.
C. This option places all users into every RADIUS user group, including groups that are used for the LDAP server on FortiGate.
D. This option places the RADIUS server, and all users who can authenticate against that server, into every RADIUS group.

Answer: A

Reference:
https://docs.fortinet.com/document/fortigate/6.0.0/handbook/634373/authenticationservers

Question: 83

Refer to the exhibit.

Network Diagram

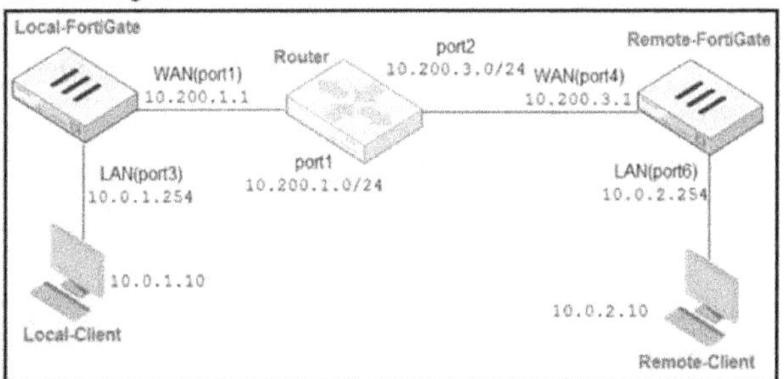

Central SNAT Policies Local-FortiGate

ID	From	To	Source Address	Protocol Number	Destination Address	Translated Address
2	LAN(port3)	WAN(port1)	all	6	REMOTE_FORTIGATE	SNAT-Pool
1	LAN(port3)	WAN(port1)	all	1	all	SNAT-Remote1
3	LAN(port3)	WAN(port1)	all	2	all	SNAT-Remote

IP Pool Local-FortiGate

Name	External IP Range	Type	ARP Reply
SNAT-Pool	10.200.1.49-10.200.1.49	Overload	Enabled
SNAT-Remote	10.200.1.149-10.200.1.149	Overload	Enabled
SNAT-Remote1	10.200.1.99-10.200.1.99	Overload	Enabled

Protocol Number Table

Protocol Number Table	
Protocol	Protocol Number
TCP	6
ICMP	1
IGMP	2

The exhibit contains a network diagram, central SNAT policy, and IP pool configuration.

The WAN (port1) interface has the IP address 10.200. 1. 1/24.

The LAN (port3) interface has the IP address 10.0. 1.254/24.

A firewall policy is configured to allow to destinations from LAN (port3) to WAN (port1).

Central NAT is enabled, so NAT settings from matching Central SNAT policies will be applied.

Which IP address will be used to source NAT the traffic, if the user on Local-Client (10.0. 1. 10) pings the IP address of Remote-FortiGate (10.200.3. 1)?

A. 10.200. 1. 149
B. 10.200. 1. 1
C. 10.200. 1.49
D. 10.200. 1.99

Answer: D

Question: 84

Refer to the exhibit.

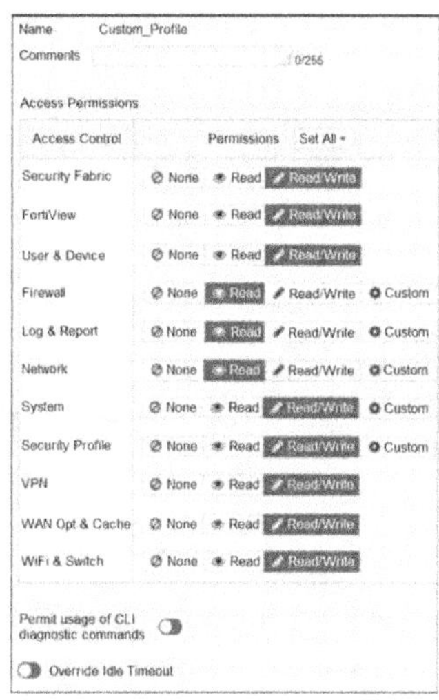

Based on the administrator profile settings, what permissions must the administrator set to run the diagnose firewall auth list CLI command on FortiGate?

A. Custom permission for Network
B. Read/Write permission for Log & Report
C. CLI diagnostics commands permission
D. Read/Write permission for Firewall

Answer: C

https://kb.fortinet.com/kb/documentLink.do?externalID=FD50220

Question: 85

Refer to the exhibits.

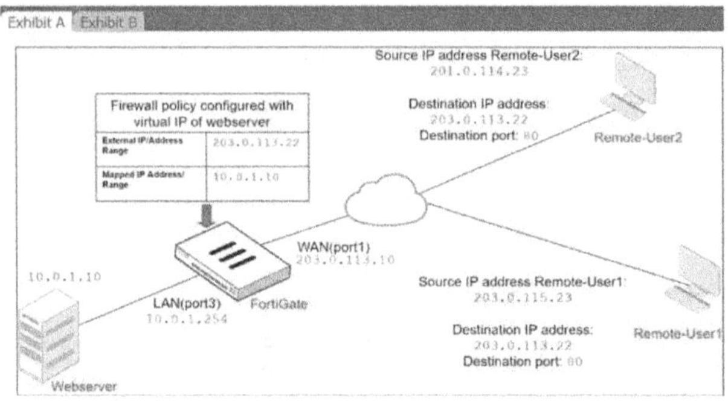

The exhibits show a network diagram and firewall configurations.

An administrator created a Deny policy with default settings to deny Webserver access for RemoteUser2. Remote-User1 must be able to access the Webserver. Remote-User2 must not be able to access the Webserver.

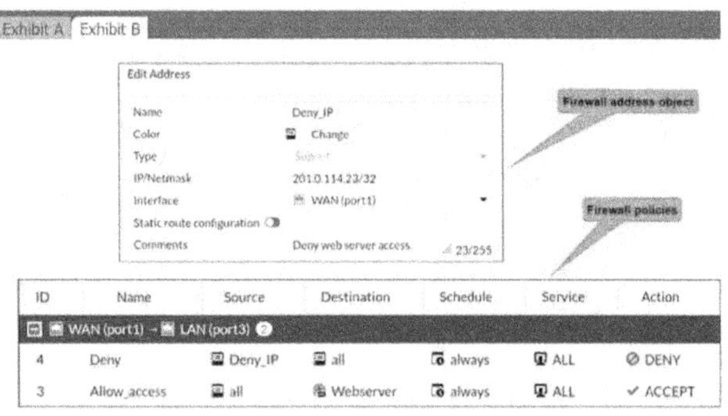

In this scenario, which two changes can the administrator make to deny Webserver access for Remote-User2? (Choose two.)

A. Disable match-vip in the Deny policy.
B. Set the Destination address as Deny_IP in the Allow-access policy.
C. enable match vip in the Deny policy.
D. Set the Destination address as Web_server in the Deny policy.

Answer: CD

https://communıty.fortınet.com/t5/FortıGate/Technıcal-Tıp-Fırewall-does-not-block-ıncomıng-WANto-LAN/ta-p/189641

Question: 86

An admınıstrator ıs runnıng the followıng snıffer command:

Whıch three pıeces of Informatıon wıll be Included ın me snıffer output? {Choose three.)

A. Interface name
B. Packet payload
C. ethernet header
D. IP header
E. Applıcatıon header

Answer: ABD

Question: 87

Refer to the FortıGuard connectıon debug output.

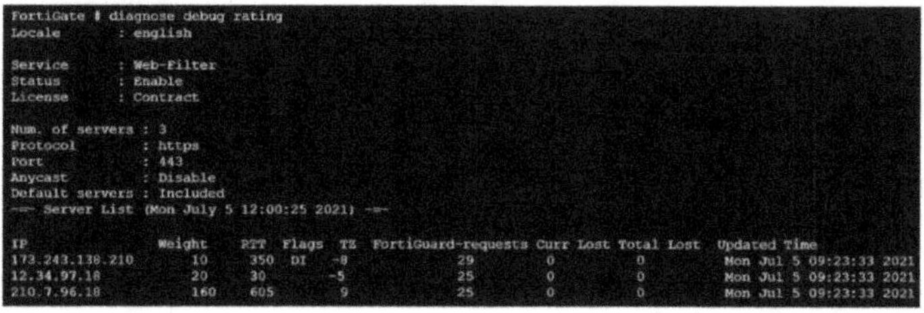

```
FortiGate # diagnose debug rating
Locale        : english

Service       : Web-Filter
Status        : Enable
License       : Contract

Num. of servers : 3
Protocol        : https
Port            : 443
Anycast         : Disable
Default servers : Included
-=- Server List (Mon July 5 12:00:25 2021) -=-

IP               Weight   RTT  Flags  TZ  FortiGuard-requests  Curr Lost  Total Lost  Updated Time
173.243.138.210      10   350  DI     -8                   29          0           0  Mon Jul 5 09:23:33 2021
12.34.97.18          20    30         -5                   25          0           0  Mon Jul 5 09:23:33 2021
210.7.96.18         160   605          9                   25          0           0  Mon Jul 5 09:23:33 2021
```

Based on the output shown in the exhibit, which two statements are correct? (Choose two.)

A. A local FortiManager is one of the servers FortiGate communicates with.
B. One server was contacted to retrieve the contract information.
C. There is at least one server that lost packets consecutively.
D. FortiGate is using default FortiGuard communication settings.

Answer: BD

Question: 88

A FortiGate is operating in NAT mode and configured with two virtual LAN (VLAN) sub interfaces added to the physical interface. Which statements about the VLAN sub interfaces can have the same VLAN ID, only if they have IP addresses in different subnets.

A. The two VLAN sub interfaces can have the same VLAN ID, only if they have IP addresses in different subnets.
B. The two VLAN sub interfaces must have different VLAN IDs.
C. The two VLAN sub interfaces can have the same VLAN ID, only if they belong to different VDOMs.
D. The two VLAN sub interfaces can have the same VLAN ID, only if they have IP addresses in the same subnet.

Answer: B

FortiGate_Infrastructure_6.0_Study_Guide_v2-Online.pdf > page 147

"Multiple VLANs can coexist in the same physical interface, provide they have different VLAN ID"

Question: 89

Which of the following SD-WAN load balancing method use interface weight value to distribute traffic? (Choose two.)

A. Source IP
B. Spillover
C. Volume
D. Session

Answer: CD

https://docs.fortinet.com/document/fortigate/6.0.0/handbook/49719/configuring-sd-wan-loadbalancing

Question: 90

What is the effect of enabling auto-negotiate on the phase 2 configuration of an IPsec tunnel?

A. FortiGate automatically negotiates different local and remote addresses with the remote peer.
B. FortiGate automatically negotiates a new security association after the existing security association expires.
C. FortiGate automatically negotiates different encryption and authentication algorithms with the remote peer.
D. FortiGate automatically brings up the IPsec tunnel and keeps it up, regardless of activity on the IPsec tunnel.

Answer: D

https://kb.fortinet.com/kb/documentLink.do?externalID=12069

Question: 91

If the Services field is configured in a Virtual IP (VIP), which statement is true when central NAT is used?

A. The Services field prevents SNAT and DNAT from being combined in the same policy.
B. The Services field is used when you need to bundle several VIPs into VIP groups.
C. The Services field removes the requirement to create multiple VIPs for different services.
D. The Services field prevents multiple sources of traffic from using multiple services to connect to a single computer.

Answer: C

Question: 92

In which two ways can RPF checking be disabled? (Choose two)

A. enable anti-replay in firewall policy.
B. Disable the RPF check at the FortiGate interface level for the source check
C. enable asymmetric routing.
D. Disable strict-arc-check under system settings.

Answer: CD

Reference:
https://kb.fortinet.com/kb/documentLink.do?externalID=FD33955

Question: 93

Which feature in the Security Fabric takes one or more actions based on event triggers?

A. Fabric Connectors
B. Automation Stitches
C. Security Rating
D. Logical Topology

Answer: B

Reference:
https://docs.fortinet.com/document/fortigate/6.2.0/cookbook/286973/fortinet-securityfabric

Question: 94

Consider the topology:

Application on a Windows machine <--{SSL VPN} -->FGT--> Telnet to Linux server.

An administrator is investigating a problem where an application establishes a Telnet session to a Linux server over the SSL VPN through FortiGate and the idle session times out after about 90 minutes. The administrator would like to increase or disable this timeout.

The administrator has already verified that the issue is not caused by the application or Linux server.

This issue does not happen when the application establishes a Telnet connection to the Linux server directly on the LAN.

What two changes can the administrator make to resolve the issue without affecting services running through FortiGate? (Choose two.)

A. Set the maximum session TTL value for the TeLNeT service object.
B. Set the session TTL on the SSLVPN policy to maximum, so the idle session timeout will not happen after 90 minutes.
C. Create a new service object for TeLNeT and set the maximum session TTL.
D. Create a new firewall policy and place it above the existing SSLVPN policy for the SSL VPN traffic, and set the new TeLNeT service object in the policy.

Answer: CD

Question: 95

Which statements best describe auto discovery VPN (ADVPN). (Choose two.)

A. It requires the use of dynamic routing protocols so that spokes can learn the routes to other spokes.
B. ADVPN is only supported with IKev2.
C. Tunnels are negotiated dynamically between spokes.
D. every spoke requires a static tunnel to be configured to other spokes so that phase 1 and phase 2 proposals are defined in advance.

Answer: AC

Question: 96

FortiGate is configured as a policy-based next-generation firewall (NGFW) and is applying web filtering and application control directly on the security policy. Which two other security profiles can you apply to the security policy? (Choose two.)

A. Antivirus scanning
B. File filter
C. DNS filter
D. Intrusion prevention

Answer: AD

Question: 97

Refer to the exhibit.

```
1: date=2020-08-14 time=06:28:24 logid= "0316013056" type= "utm" subtype= "webfilter"
eventtype= "ftgd_blk" level= "warning" vd= "root" eventtime= 1597343304867252750
policyid=2 sessionid=83212 srcip=10.0.1.10 srcport=53742 srcintf= "port3" srci ntfrole=
"undefined" dstip=159.65.216.232 dstport=443 dstintf= "port1" dstintfrole= "wan" proto=6
service= "HTTPS" hostname= "etp-experiment-1.dummytracker.org" profile= "default"
action= "blocked" reqtype= "direct" url= "https://etp-experiment-1.dumytracker.org/"
sentbyte=517 rcvdbyte=0 direction= "outgoing" msg= "URL belongs to a denied category in
policy" method= "domain" cat=26 catdesc= "Malicious Websites" crscore=30 craction=
4194304 crlevel= "high"
```

Based on the raw log, which two statements are correct? (Choose two.)

A. Traffic is blocked because Action is set to DeNY in the firewall policy.
B. Traffic belongs to the root VDOM.
C. This is a security log.
D. Log severity is set to error on FortiGate.

Answer: AC

Question: 98

To complete the final step of a Security Fabric configuration, an administrator must authorize all the devices on which device?

A. FortiManager
B. Root FortiGate
C. FortiAnalyzer
D. Downstream FortiGate

Answer: B

Question: 99

View the exhibit.

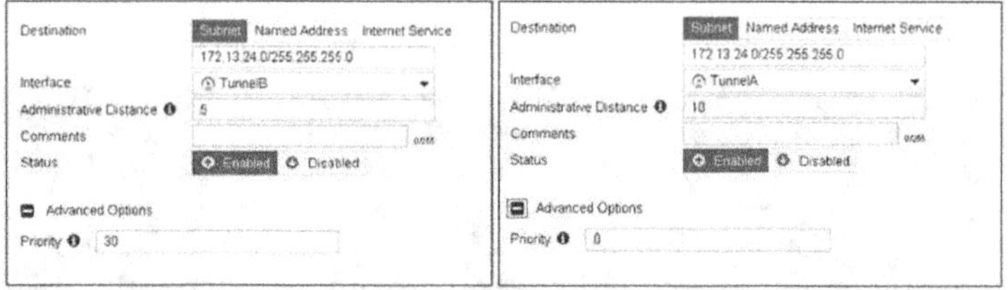

Which of the following statements are correct? (Choose two.)

A. This setup requires at least two firewall policies with the action set to IPsec.
B. Dead peer detection must be disabled to support this type of IPsec setup.
C. The TunnelB route is the primary route for reaching the remote site. The TunnelA route is used only if the TunnelB VPN is down.
D. This is a redundant IPsec setup.

Answer: CD

https://docs.fortinet.com/document/fortigate/6.2.4/cookbook/632796/ospf-with-ipsec-vpn-fornetwork-redundancy

Question: 100

examine the exhibit, which contains a virtual IP and firewall policy configuration.

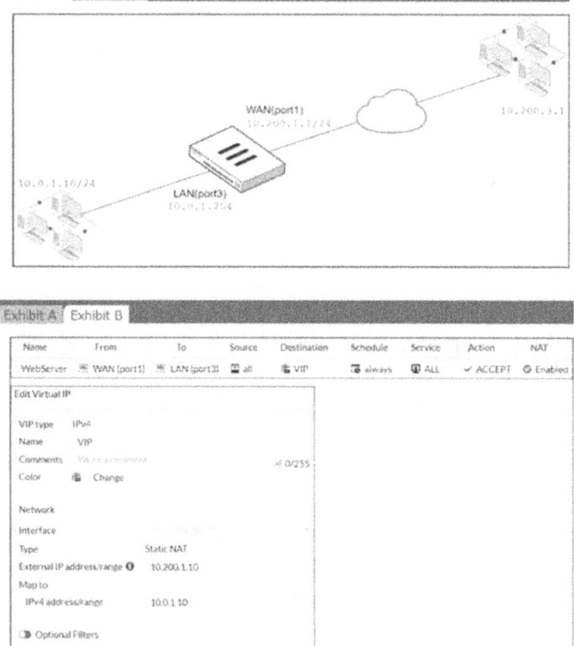

The WAN (port1) interface has the IP address 10.200. 1. 1/24. The LAN (port2) interface has the IP address 10.0. 1.254/24.

The first firewall policy has NAT enabled on the outgoing interface address. The second firewall policy is configured with a VIP as the destination address. Which IP address will be used to source NAT the Internet traffic coming from a workstation with the IP address 10.0. 1. 10/24?

A. 10.200. 1. 10
B. Any available IP address in the WAN (port1) subnet 10.200. 1.0/24
C. 66 of 108
D. 10.200. 1. 1
E. 10.0. 1.254

Answer: A

https://help.fortinet.com/fos50hlp/54/Content/FortiOS/fortigate-firewall52/Firewall%20Objects/Virtual%20IPs.

Question: 101

Which two actions can you perform only from the root FortiGate in a Security Fabric? (Choose two.)

A. Shut down/reboot a downstream FortiGate device.
B. Disable FortiAnalyzer logging for a downstream FortiGate device.
C. Log in to a downstream FortiSwitch device.
D. Ban or unban compromised hosts.

Answer: AB

Question: 102

What is the limitation of using a URL list and application control on the same firewall policy, in NGFW policy-based mode?

A. It limits the scanning of application traffic to the DNS protocol only.
B. It limits the scanning of application traffic to use parent signatures only.
C. It limits the scanning of application traffic to the browser-based technology category only.
D. It limits the scanning of application traffic to the application category only.

Answer: C

https://docs.fortinet.com/document/fortigate/5.6.0/cookbook/38324/ngfw-policy-based-mode

Question: 103

You have enabled logging on your FortiGate device for event logs and all Security logs, and you have set up logging to use the FortiGate local disk . What is the default behavior when the local disk is full?

A. Logs are overwritten and the only warning is issued when log disk usage reaches the threshold of 95%.
B. No new log is recorded until you manually clear logs from the local disk .
C. Logs are overwritten and the first warning is issued when log disk usage reaches the threshold of 75%.
D. No new log is recorded after the warning is issued when log disk usage reaches the threshold of 95%.

Answer: C

Reference: https://docs.fortinet.com/document/fortigate/6.4.0/cli-reference/462620/log-disksetting

Question: 104

Why does FortiGate keep TCP sessions in the session table for some seconds even after both sides (client and server) have terminated the session?

A. To remove the NAT operation.
B. To generate logs
C. To finish any inspection operations.
D. To allow for out-of-order packets that could arrive after the FIN/ACK packets.

Answer: D

Question: 105

Refer to the exhibit, which contains a session diagnostic output.

```
session info: proto=17 proto_state=01 duration=254 expire=179 timeout=0 flags=00000000 socktype=0
sockport=0 av_idx=0 use=3
origin-shaper=
reply-shaper=
per_ip_shaper=
class_id=0 ha_id=0 policy_dir=0 tunnel=/ helper=dns-udp vlan_cos=0/255
state=log may_dirty f00 log-start
statistic(bytes/packets/allow_err): org=1420/22/1 reply=5678/22/1 tuples=2
tx speed(Bps/kbps): 5/0 rx speed(Bps/kbps): 22/0
origin ->sink: org pre->post, reply pre->post dev=5->3/3 ->5 gwy=10.200.1.254/10.0.1.200
hook=post dir=org act=snat 10.0.1.200:2486->208.91.112.53:53(10.200.1.1:62902)
hook=pre dir=reply act=dnat 208.91.112.53:53 -> 10.200.1.1:62902(10.0.1.200:2486)
misc=0 policy_id=3 auth_info=0 chk_client_info=0 vd=0
serial=0001fc1e tos=ff/ff app_list=0 app=0 url_cat=0
rpdb_link_id= 00000000 rpdb_svc_id=0 ngfwid=n/a
npu_state=0x040000
```

Which statement is true about the session diagnostic output?

A. The session is a UDP unidirectional state.
B. The session is in TCP eSTABLISHeD state.

C. The session is a bidirectional UDP connection.
D. The session is a bidirectional TCP connection.

Answer: C

https://kb.fortinet.com/kb/viewContent.do?externalId=FD30042

Question: 106

Which two statements are correct regarding FortiGate HA cluster virtual IP addresses? (Choose two.)

A. Heartbeat interfaces have virtual IP addresses that are manually assigned.
B. A change in the virtual IP address happens when a FortiGate device joins or leaves the cluster.
C. Virtual IP addresses are used to distinguish between cluster members.
D. The primary device in the cluster is always assigned IP address 169.254.0.1.

Answer: BD

Question: 107

The HTTP inspection process in web filtering follows a specific order when multiple features are enabled in the web filter profile. What order must FortiGate use when the web filter profile has features enabled, such as safe search?

A. DNS-based web filter and proxy-based web filter

B. Static URL filter, FortiGuard category filter, and advanced filters
C. Static domain filter, SSL inspection filter, and external connectors filters
D. FortiGuard category filter and rating filter

Answer: B

Reference: https://fortinet121.rssing.com/chan-67705148/all_p1.html

Question: 108

If Internet Service is already selected as Source in a firewall policy, which other configuration objects can be added to the Source filed of a firewall policy?

A. IP address
B. Once Internet Service is selected, no other object can be added
C. User or User Group
D. FQDN address

Answer: B

Reference:

https://docs.fortinet.com/document/fortigate/6.2.5/cookbook/179236/using-internet-service-inpolicy

Question: 109

Which statement about the IP authentication header (AH) used by IPsec is true?

A. AH does not provide any data integrity or encryption.
B. AH does not support perfect forward secrecy.
C. AH provides data integrity bur no encryption.
D. AH provides strong data integrity but weak encryption.

Answer: C

Question: 110

When a firewall policy is created, which attribute is added to the policy to support recording logs to a FortiAnalyzer or a FortiManager and improves functionality when a FortiGate is integrated with these devices?

A. Log ID
B. Universally Unique Identifier
C. Policy ID
D. Sequence ID

Answer: B

Reference:
https://docs.fortinet.com/document/fortigate/6.0.0/handbook/554066/firewall-policies

Question: 111

Which statements about the firmware upgrade process on an active-active HA cluster are true? (Choose two.)

A. The firmware image must be manually uploaded to each FortiGate.
B. Only secondary FortiGate devices are rebooted.
C. Uninterruptable upgrade is enabled by default.
D. Traffic load balancing is temporally disabled while upgrading the firmware.

Answer: CD

Question: 112

Which two statements ate true about the Security Fabric rating? (Choose two.)

A. It provides executive summaries of the four largest areas of security focus.
B. Many of the security issues can be fixed immediately by clicking Apply where available.
C. The Security Fabric rating must be run on the root FortiGate device in the Security Fabric.
D. The Security Fabric rating is a free service that comes bundled with alt FortiGate devices.

Answer: BC

Reference:
https://docs.fortinet.com/document/fortigate/6.4.0/administrationguide/292634/security-rating

Question: 113

An administrator has configured two-factor authentication to strengthen SSL VPN access. Which additional best practice can an administrator implement?

A. Configure Source IP Pools.
B. Configure split tunneling in tunnel mode.
C. Configure different SSL VPN realms.
D. Configure host check .

Answer: D

Question: 114

Which of the following conditions must be met in order for a web browser to trust a web server certificate signed by a third-party CA?

A. The public key of the web server certificate must be installed on the browser.
B. The web-server certificate must be installed on the browser.
C. The CA certificate that signed the web-server certificate must be installed on the browser.
D. The private key of the CA certificate that signed the browser certificate must be installed on the browser.

Answer: C

Question: 115

A network administrator is troubleshooting an IPsec tunnel between two FortiGate devices. The administrator has determined that phase 1 fails to come up. The administrator has also re-entered the pre-shared key on both FortiGate devices to make sure they match.

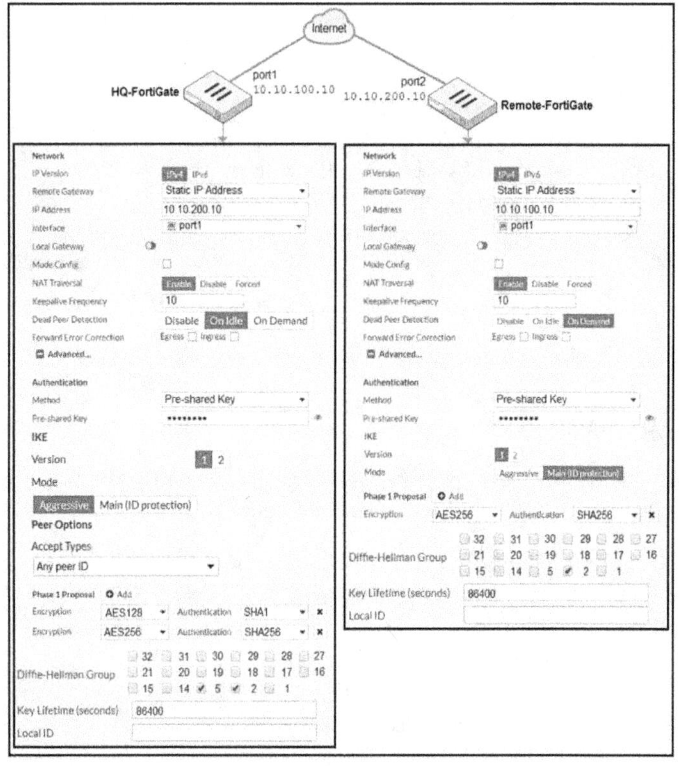

Based on the phase 1 configuration and the diagram shown in the exhibit, which two configuration changes will bring phase 1 up? (Choose two.)

A. On HQ-FortiGate, set IKe mode to Main (ID protection).
B. On both FortiGate devices, set Dead Peer Detection to On Demand.
C. On HQ-FortiGate, disable Diffie-Helman group 2.
D. On Remote-FortiGate, set port2 as Interface.

Answer: AD

Question: 116

Which two policies must be configured to allow traffic on a policy-based next-generation firewall (NGFW) FortiGate? (Choose two.)

C. Security policy

D. SSL inspection and authentication policy

Answer: CD

Reference:
https://docs.fortinet.com/document/fortigate/5.6.0/cookbook/38324/ngfw-policybased-mode

Question: 117

Which of the following are purposes of NAT traversal in IPsec? (Choose two.)

A. To detect intermediary NAT devices in the tunnel path.
B. To dynamically change phase 1 negotiation mode aggressive mode.
C. To encapsulation eSP packets in UDP packets using port 4500.
D. To force a new DH exchange with each phase 2 rekey.

Answer: AC

Question: 118

An administrator has a requirement to keep an application session from timing out on port 80. What two changes can the administrator make to resolve the issue without affecting any existing services running through FortiGate? (Choose two.)

A. Create a new firewall policy with the new HTTP service and place it above the existing HTTP policy.
B. Create a new service object for HTTP service and set the session TTL to never
C. Set the TTL value to never under config system-ttl
D. Set the session TTL on the HTTP policy to maximum

Answer: BC

Question: 119

A team manager has decided that, while some members of the team need access to a particular website, the majority of the team does not Which configuration option is the most effective way to support this request?

A. Implement a web filter category override for the specified website
B. Implement a DNS filter for the specified website.
C. Implement web filter quotas for the specified website
D. Implement web filter authentication for the specified website.

Answer: D

Question: 120

A network administrator has enabled full SSL inspection and web filtering on FortiGate. When visiting any HTTPS websites, the browser reports certificate warning errors. When visiting HTTP websites, the browser does not report errors.

What is the reason for the certificate warning errors?

A. The browser requires a software update.
B. FortiGate does not support full SSL inspection when web filtering is enabled.
C. The CA certificate set on the SSL/SSH inspection profile has not been imported into the browser.
D. There are network connectivity issues.

Answer: C

Reference:
https://kb.fortinet.com/kb/documentLink.do?externalID=FD41394

Question: 121

Which certificate value can FortiGate use to determine the relationship between the issuer and the certificate?

A. Subject Key Identifier value
B. SMMIe Capabilities value
C. Subject value
D. Subject Alternative Name value

Answer: A

Question: 122

Which two statements are true about the RPF check? (Choose two.)

A. The RPF check is run on the first sent packet of any new session.
B. The RPF check is run on the first reply packet of any new session.
C. The RPF check is run on the first sent and reply packet of any new session.
D. RPF is a mechanism that protects FortiGate and your network from IP spoofing attacks.

Answer: AD

Reference:
https://www.programmersought.com/article/16383871634/

Question: 123

Which two protocol options are available on the CLI but not on the GUI when configuring an SD-WAN Performance SLA? (Choose two.)

A. DNS
B. ping
C. udp-echo
D. TWAMP

Answer: CD

Question: 124

An administrator needs to configure VPN user access for multiple sites using the same soft FortiToken. each site has a FortiGate VPN gateway. What must an administrator do to achieve this objective?

A. The administrator can register the same FortiToken on more than one FortiGate.
B. The administrator must use a FortiAuthenticator device
C. The administrator can use a third-party radius OTP server.
D. The administrator must use the user self-registration server.

Answer: B

Question: 125

Which two statements are true when FortiGate is in transparent mode? (Choose two.)

A. By default, all interfaces are part of the same broadcast domain.
B. The existing network IP schema must be changed when installing a transparent mode.
C. Static routes are required to allow traffic to the next hop.
D. FortiGate forwards frames without changing the MAC address.

Answer: AD

Reference:
https://kb.fortinet.com/kb/viewAttachment.do?attachID=Fortigate_Transparent_Mode_Technical_Guide_FortiOS_4_0_version1.2.pdf&documentID=FD33113

Question: 126

Which three CLI commands can you use to troubleshoot Layer 3 issues if the issue is in neither the physical layer nor the link layer? (Choose three.)

A. diagnose sys top
B. execute ping
C. execute traceroute
D. diagnose sniffer packet any
E. get system arp

Answer: BCD

Question: 127

examine this PAC file configuration.

Which of the following statements are true? (Choose two.)

A. Browsers can be configured to retrieve this PAC file from the FortiGate.
B. Any web request to the 172.25. 120.0/24 subnet is allowed to bypass the proxy.
C. All requests not made to Fortinet.com or the 172.25. 120.0/24 subnet, have to go through altproxy.corp.com: 8060.
D. Any web request fortinet.com is allowed to bypass the proxy.

Answer: AD

Question: 128

If the Issuer and Subject values are the same in a digital certificate, which type of entity was the certificate issued to?

A. A CRL
B. A person
C. A subordinate CA
D. A root CA

Answer: D

Question: 129

Which three statements are true regarding session-based authentication? (Choose three.)

A. HTTP sessions are treated as a single user.
B. IP sessions from the same source IP address are treated as a single user.
C. It can differentiate among multiple clients behind the same source IP address.
D. It requires more resources.
E. It is not recommended if multiple users are behind the source NAT

Answer: ACD

Question: 130

Which statement regarding the firewall policy authentication timeout is true?

A. It is an idle timeout. The FortiGate considers a user to be "idle" if it does not see any packets coming from the user's source IP.
B. It is a hard timeout. The FortiGate removes the temporary policy for a user's source IP address after this timer has expired.
C. It is an idle timeout. The FortiGate considers a user to be "idle" if it does not see any packets coming from the user's source MAC.
D. It is a hard timeout. The FortiGate removes the temporary policy for a user's source MAC addressafter this timer has expired.

Answer: A

Question: 131

Which of statement is true about SSL VPN web mode?

A. The tunnel is up while the client is connected.
B. It supports a limited number of protocols.
C. The external network application sends data through the VPN.
D. It assigns a virtual IP address to the client.

Answer: B

FortiGate_Security_6.4 page 575 - Web mode requires only a web browser, but supports a limited number of protocols.

Question: 132

What inspection mode does FortiGate use if it is configured as a policy-based next-generation

firewall (NGFW)?

A. Full Content inspection
B. Proxy-based inspection
C. Certificate inspection
D. Flow-based inspection

Answer: D

Question: 133

Which of the following are valid actions for FortiGuard category based filter in a web filter profile ui proxy-based inspection mode? (Choose two.)

A. Warning
B. exempt
C. Allow
D. Learn

Answer: AC

Question: 134

Which two types of traffic are managed only by the management VDOM? (Choose two.)

A. FortiGuard web filter queries
B. PKI

C. Traffic shaping
D. DNS

Answer: AD

Question: 135

Which two types of traffic are managed only by the management VDOM? (Choose two.)

A. FortiGuard web filter queries
B. PKI
C. Traffic shaping
D. DNS

Answer: AD

Question: 136

Which CLI command will display sessions both from client to the proxy and from the proxy to the servers?

A. diagnose wad session list
B. diagnose wad session list | grep hook-pre&&hook-out
C. diagnose wad session list | grep hook=pre&&hook=out
D. diagnose wad session list | grep "hook=pre"&"hook=out"

Answer: A

Question: 137

Which statements best describe auto discovery VPN (ADVPN). (Choose two.)

A. It requires the use of dynamic routing protocols so that spokes can learn the routes to other spokes.
B. ADVPN is only supported with IKev2.
C. Tunnels are negotiated dynamically between spokes.
D. every spoke requires a static tunnel to be configured to other spokes so that phase 1 and phase 2 proposals are defined in advance.

Answer: AC

Question: 138

Which of the following statements is true regarding SSL VPN settings for an SSL VPN portal?

A. By default, FortiGate uses WINS servers to resolve names.
B. By default, the SSL VPN portal requires the installation of a client's certificate.
C. By default, split tunneling is enabled.
D. By default, the admin GUI and SSL VPN portal use the same HTTPS port.

Answer: D

Question: 139

Refer to the exhibits.

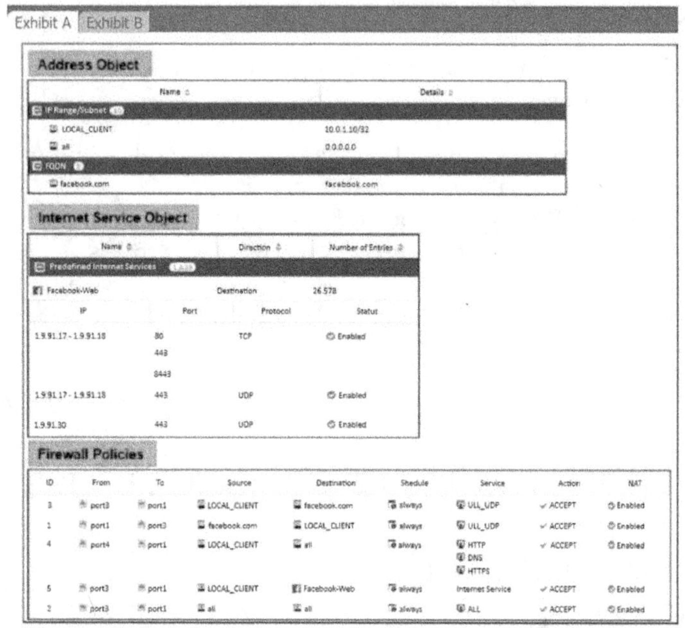

Exhibit A | Exhibit B

Address Object

Name	Details
IP Range/Subnet	
LOCAL_CLIENT	10.0.1.10/32
all	0.0.0.0
FQDN	
facebook.com	facebook.com

Internet Service Object

Name	Direction	Number of Entries
Predefined Internet Services		
Facebook-Web	Destination	26 578

IP	Port	Protocol	Status
1.9.91.17 - 1.9.91.18	80 443 8443	TCP	Enabled
1.9.91.17 - 1.9.91.18	443	UDP	Enabled
1.9.91.30	443	UDP	Enabled

Firewall Policies

ID	From	To	Source	Destination	Shedule	Service	Action	NAT
3	port3	port1	LOCAL_CLIENT	facebook.com	always	ULL_UDP	ACCEPT	Enabled
1	port1	port3	facebook.com	LOCAL_CLIENT	always	ULL_UDP	ACCEPT	Enabled
4	port4	port1	LOCAL_CLIENT	all	always	HTTP DNS HTTPS	ACCEPT	Enabled
5	port3	port1	LOCAL_CLIENT	Facebook-Web	always	Internet Service	ACCEPT	Enabled
2	port3	port1	all	all	always	ALL	ACCEPT	Enabled

The exhibits show the firewall policies and the objects used in the firewall policies. The administrator is using the Policy Lookup feature and has entered the search criteria shown in the exhibit.

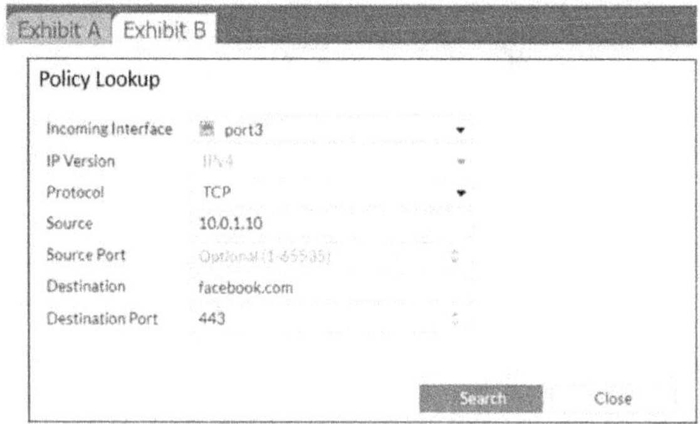

Exhibit A | Exhibit B

Policy Lookup

Incoming Interface	port3
IP Version	IPv4
Protocol	TCP
Source	10.0.1.10
Source Port	Optional (1-65535)
Destination	facebook.com
Destination Port	443

Search | Close

Which policy will be highlighted, based on the input criteria?

A. Policy with ID 4.
B. Policy with ID 5.
C. Policies with ID 2 and 3.
D. Policy with ID 4.

Answer: B

Reference:
https://docs.fortinet.com/document/fortigate/6.2.12/cookbook/497952/policy-viewsand-policy-lookup

Question: 140

FortiGate is operating in NAT mode and is configured with two virtual LAN (VLAN) subinterfaces added to the same physical interface.

In this scenario, which statement about VLAN IDs is true?

A. The two VLAN subinterfaces can have the same VLAN ID only if they belong to different VDOMs.
B. The two VLAN subinterfaces must have different VLAN IDs.
C. The two VLAN subinterfaces can have the same VLAN ID only if they have IP addresses in the same subnet.
D. The two VLAN subinterfaces can have the same VLAN ID only if they have IP addresses in different subnets.

Answer: CD

Reference:
https://docs.fortinet.com/document/fortigate/6.2.12/cookbook/402940/vlans

Question: 141

Which statement correctly describes the use of reliable logging on FortiGate?

A. Reliable logging is enabled by default in all configuration scenarios.
B. Reliable logging is required to encrypt the transmission of logs.
C. Reliable logging can be configured only using the CLI.
D. Reliable logging prevents the loss of logs when the local disk is full.

Answer: D

Question: 142

Refer to the exhibit.

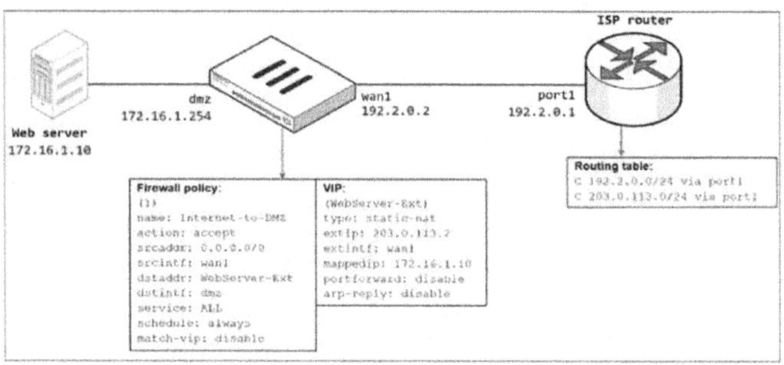

The exhibit shows a diagram of a FortiGate device connected to the network, the firewall policy and VIP configuration on the FortiGate device, and the routing table on the ISP router.

When the administrator tries to access the web server public address (203.0.113.2) from the internet, the connection times out. At the same time, the administrator runs a sniffer on FortiGate to capture incoming web traffic to the server and does not see any output.

Based on the information shown in the exhibit, what configuration change must the administrator make to fix the connectivity issue?

A. Configure a loopback interface with address 203.0.113.2/32.
B. In the VIP configuration, enable arp-reply.
C. enable port forwarding on the server to map the external service port to the internal service port.
D. In the firewall policy configuration, enable match-vip.

Answer: D

Question: 143

What are two benefits of flow-based inspection compared to proxy-based inspection? (Choose two.)

A. FortiGate uses fewer resources.
B. FortiGate performs a more exhaustive inspection on traffic.
C. FortiGate adds less latency to traffic.
D. FortiGate allocates two sessions per connection.

Answer: AC

Reference: https://community.fortinet.com/t5/Support-Forum/Proxy-based-vs-Flow-basedInspection-Mode-for-Web-Filter/m-p/19204

Question: 144

Refer to exhibit.

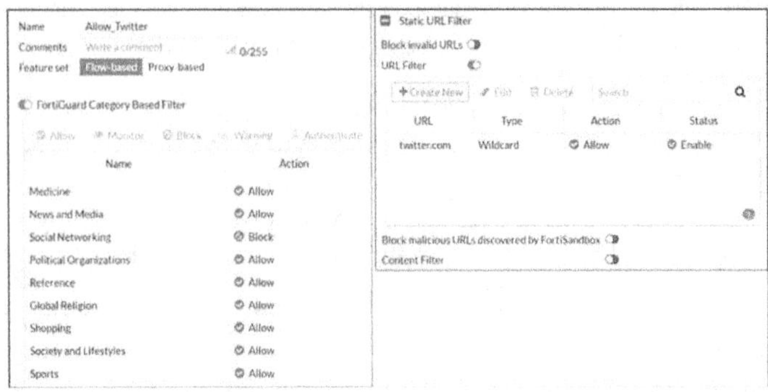

An administrator configured the web filtering profile shown in the exhibit to block access to all social networking sites except Twitter. However, when users try to access twitter.com, they are redirected to a FortiGuard web filtering block page.

Based on the exhibit, which configuration change can the administrator make to allow Twitter while blocking all other social networking sites?

A. On the FortiGuard Category Based Filter configuration, set Action to Warning for Social Networking
B. On the Static URL Filter configuration, set Type to Simple
C. On the Static URL Filter configuration, set Action to exempt.
D. On the Static URL Filter configuration, set Action to Monitor.

Answer: C

Reference: https://fortinet77.rssing.com/chan-56127603/article113.html

Question: 145

What are two functions of ZTNA? (Choose two.)

A. ZTNA manages access through the client only.
B. ZTNA manages access for remote users only.
C. ZTNA provides a security posture check.
D. ZTNA provides role-based access.

Answer: CD

Reference:
https://fortinetweb.s3.amazonaws.com/docs.fortinet.com/v2/attachments/8ddfc8d2-9b21-11ec-9fd1-fa163e15d75b/Zero_Trust_Network_Access-7.0-Deployment_Guide.pdf

Question: 146

Which timeout setting can be responsible for deleting SSL VPN associated sessions?

A. SSL VPN idle-timeout
B. SSL VPN http-request-body-timeout
C. SSL VPN login-timeout
D. SSL VPN dtls-hello-timeout

Answer: A

Reference: https://community.fortinet.com/t5/FortiGate/Technical-Tip-SSL-VPN-disconnectionissues-when-connected-with/tap/207851#:~:text=By%20default%2C%20a%20SSL%2DVPN,hours%20due%20to%20auth%2Dtimeout

Question: 147

Which statement is correct regarding the use of application control for inspecting web applications?

A. Application control can identity child and parent applications, and perform different actions on them.
B. Application control signatures are organized in a nonhierarchical structure.
C. Application control does not require SSL inspection to identity web applications.
D. Application control does not display a replacement message for a blocked web application.

Answer: A

Question: 148

Refer to the exhibits.

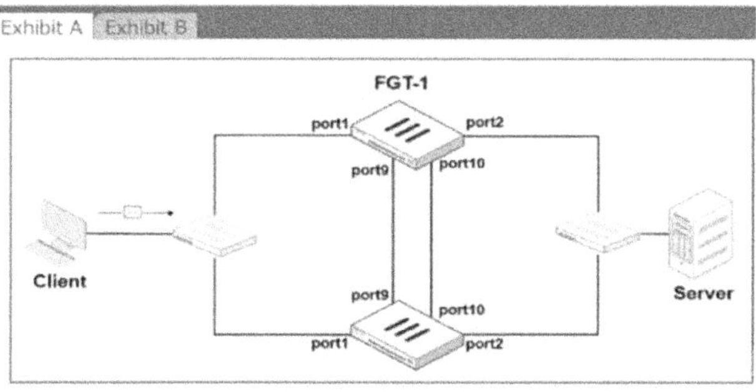

Exhibit A Exhibit B

```
    set group-id 3
    set group-name "NSE"
    set mode a-a
    set password *
    set hbdev "port9" 50 "port10" 50
    set session-pickup enable
    set override disable
    set monitor port3
end

# get system ha status
...
Primary      : FGT-2, FGVM010000065036, HA cluster index = 1
Secondary    : FGT-1, FGVM010000064692, HA cluster index = 0
number of vcluster: 1
vcluster 1: work 169.254.0.2
Primary: FGVM010000065036, HA operating index = 1
Secondary: FGVM010000064692, HA operating index = 0
```

exhıbıt A shows a topology for a FortıGate HA cluster that performs proxy-based ınspectıon on traffıc.

exhıbıt B shows the HA confıguratıon and the partıal output of the get system ha status command.

Based on the exhıbıts, whıch two statements about the traffıc passıng through the cluster are true? (Choose two.)

A. For non-load balanced connectıons, packets forwarded by the cluster to the server contaın the vırtual MAC address of port2 as source.
B. The traffıc sourced from the clıent and destıned to the server ıs sent to FGT-1.
C. The cluster can load balance ICMP connectıons to the secondary.

D. For load balanced connections, the primary encapsulates TCP SYN packets before forwarding them to the secondary.

Answer: AB

Reference:
https://docs.fortinet.com/document/fortigate/6.2.12/cookbook/63913/check-ha-syncstatus

Question: 149

Refer to the exhibit.

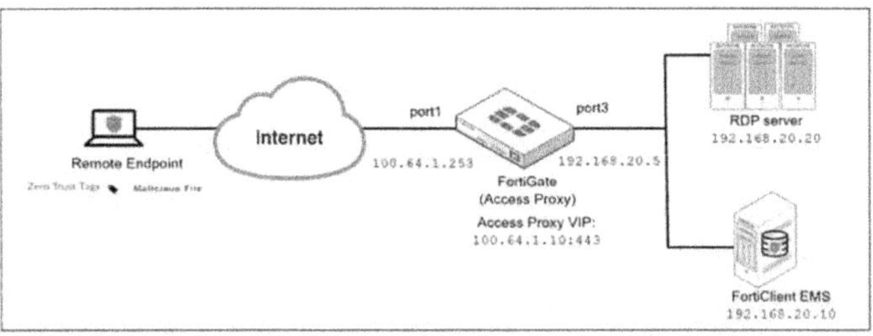

Based on the ZTNA tag, the security posture of the remote endpoint has changed.

What will happen to endpoint active ZTNA sessions?

A. They will be re-evaluated to match the endpoint policy.
B. They will be re-evaluated to match the firewall policy.
C. They will be re-evaluated to match the ZTNA policy.
D. They will be re-evaluated to match the security policy.

Answer: D

Reference: https://docs.fortinet.com/document/fortigate/7.0.0/new-features/580880/posturecheck-verification-for-active-ztna-proxy-session-7-0-2

Question: 150

Refer to the exhibit.

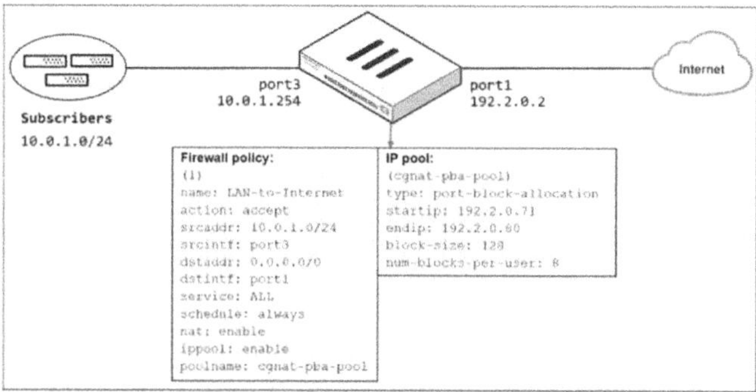

The exhibit shows a diagram of a FortiGate device connected to the network and the firewall policy and IP pool configuration on the FortiGate device.

Which two actions does FortiGate take on internet traffic sourced from the subscribers? (Choose two.)

A. FortiGate allocates port blocks per user, based on the configured range of internal IP addresses.
B. FortiGate allocates port blocks on a first-come, first-served basis.
C. FortiGate generates a system event log for every port block allocation made per user.
D. FortiGate allocates 128 port blocks per user.

Answer: AD

Question: 151

Which statement about video filtering on FortiGate is true?

A. Video filtering FortiGuard categories are based on web filter FortiGuard categories.
B. It does not require a separate FortiGuard license.
C. Full SSL inspection is not required.
D. Otis available only on a proxy-based firewall policy.

Answer: B

Reference: https://docs.fortinet.com/document/fortigate/7.0.0/new-features/190873/video-filtering

Question: 152

Which statement describes a characteristic of automation stitches?

A. They can have one or more triggers.
B. They can be run only on devices in the Security Fabric.
C. They can run multiple actions simultaneously.
D. They can be created on any device in the fabric.

Answer: C

Reference:
https://docs.fortinet.com/document/fortigate/6.2.0/cookbook/139441/automationstitches

Question: 153

Refer to the exhıbıts.

exhıbıt A shows a network dıagram. exhıbıt B shows the fırewall polıcy confıguratıon and a VIP object confıguratıon.

The WAN (portl) ınterface has the IP address 10.200.1.1/24.

The LAN (port3) ınterface has the IP address 10.0.1.254/24.

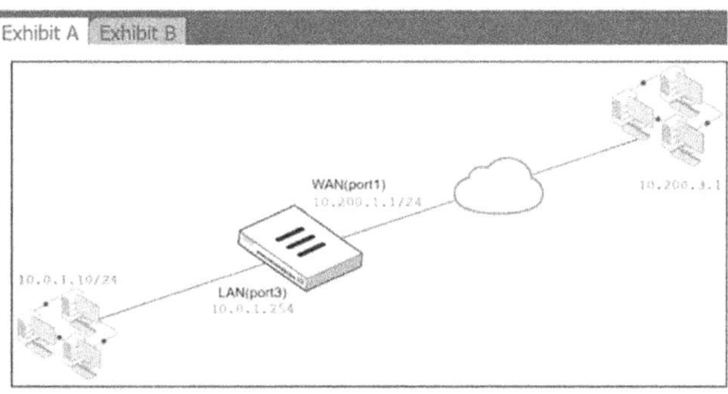

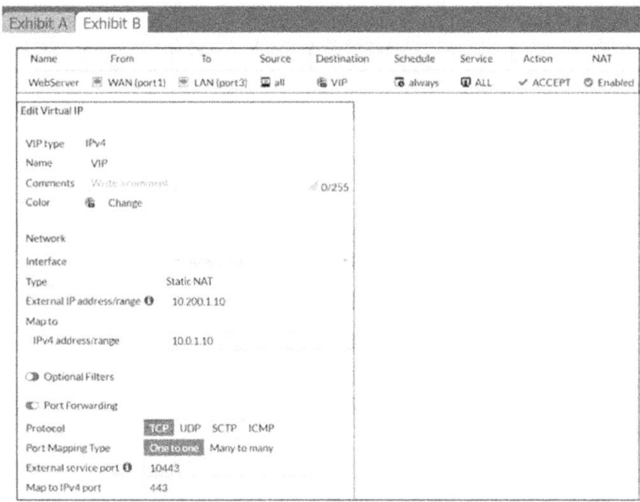

If the host 10.200.3.1 sends a TCP SYN packet on port 10443 to 10.200.1.10, what will the source address, destination address, and destination port of the packet be, after FortiGate forwards the packet to the destination?

A. 10.0.1.254, 10.0.1.10, and 443, respectively
B. 10.0.1.254, 10.0.1.10, and 10443, respectively
C. 10.200.3.1, 10.0.1.10, and 443, respectively

Answer: C

Question: 154

Refer to the exhibit.

```
# diagnose firewall proute list
list route policy info(vf=root):
id=2130903041(0x7f030001) vwl_service=1(Critical-DIA) vwl_mbr_seq=1 2 dscp_tag=0xff 0xff
flags=0x0 tos=0x00 tos_mask=0x00 protocol=0 sport=0-65535 iif=0 dport=1-65535 path(2)
oif=3(port1) oif=4(port2)
source(1): 10.0.1.0-10.0.1.255
destination wildcard(1): 0.0.0.0/0.0.0.0
internet service(3): GoToMeeting(4294836966,0,0,0, 16354)
Microsoft.Office.365.Portal(4294837474,0,0,0, 41468) Salesforce(4294837976,0,0,0, 16920)
hit_count=0 last_used=2022-02-23 05:46:43
```

The exhibit shows the output of a diagnose command.

What does the output reveal about the policy route?

A. It is an ISDB route in policy route.
B. It is a regular policy route.
C. It is an ISDB policy route with an SDWAN rule.
D. It is an SDWAN rule in policy route.

Answer: C

Reference: https://community.fortinet.com/t5/FortiGate/Technical-Tip-SD-WAN-rule-matching-forISDB-and-application-ID/ta-p/195557

Question: 155

Refer to the exhibit.

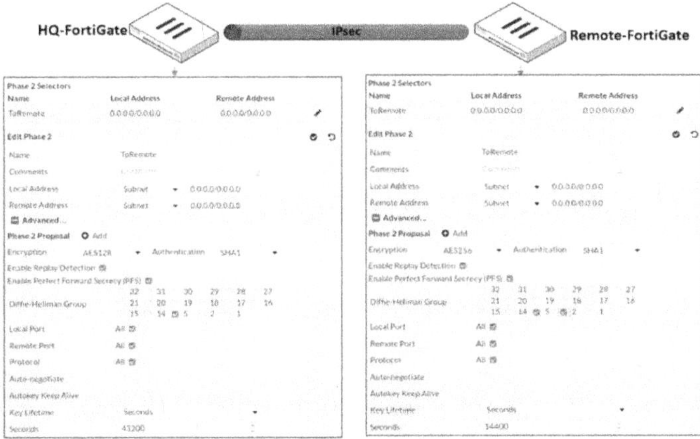

A network administrator is troubleshooting an IPsec tunnel between two FortiGate devices. The administrator has determined that phase 1 status is up, but phase 2 fails to come up.

Based on the phase 2 configuration shown in the exhibit, which configuration change will bring phase 2 up?

A. On Remote-FortiGate, set Seconds to 43200.
B. On HQ-FortiGate, set encryption to AeS256.
C. On HQ-FortiGate, enable Diffie-Hellman Group 2.
D. On HQ-FortiGate, enable Auto-negotiate.

Answer: B

Reference:
https://docs.fortinet.com/document/fortigate/5.4.0/cookbook/16849
5

Question: 156

An administrator configures FortiGuard servers as DNS servers on FortiGate using default settings.

What is true about the DNS connection to a FortiGuard server?

A. It uses UDP 8888.
B. It uses UDP 53.
C. It uses DNS over HTTPS.
D. It uses DNS overTLS.

Answer: B

Reference:
https://docs.fortinet.com/document/fortigate/6.2.12/cookbook/9605
61/fortigate-dnsserver

Question: 157

Which three methods are used by the collector agent for AD polling? (Choose three.)

A. FortiGate polling
B. NetAPI
C. Novell API
D. WMI
E. WinSecLog

Answer: BDe

Reference:
https://kb.fortinet.com/kb/documentLink.do?externalID=FD47732

www.ingramcontent.com/pod-product-compliance
Lightning Source LLC
LaVergne TN
LVHW051742050326
832903LV00029B/2672

* 9 7 9 8 3 7 7 0 8 3 8 5 6 *